Girls in Sainik Schools and Rashtriya Military Schools

Girls in Sainik Schools and Rashtriya Military Schools

Kush Kalra

BA LL.B, LL.M

UPES Law School

Vij Books India Pvt Ltd

New Delhi (India)

Published by

Vij Books India Pvt Ltd
(Publishers, Distributors & Importers)
2/19, Ansari Road
Delhi – 110 002
Phones: 91-11-43596460
Mob: 9811094883
web: www.vijbooks.in
e-mail: contact@vijpublishing.com

Copyright © 2022, *Kush Kalra*

ISBN: 978-93-93499-65-3   (Paperback)

Acknowledgments

UPES LAW SCHOOL

Contents

Preface

Offering girls basic quality education is one sure way of giving them much greater power, of enabling them to make genuine choices over the kinds of lives they wish to lead. India has ratified the convention on the 'Rights of the Child' and the convention on the 'Elimination of All Forms of Discrimination against Women'. According to Article 21 A of the Constitution of India, right to education is now a fundamental right for the children in the age group of 6-14 years.

The Sainik Schools in their vision statement provides that – "To upgrade the schools as modern public schools offering education to children of common man and to effectively use technology to integrate with the futuristic knowledge based society of emerging globalised world." However, the school's admission practice is in total violation of its vision statement. It prohibits girls, and admits only boys[1] seeking admission.

Sainik Schools are fully residential schools, affiliated to the CBSE, conceived in 1961 by VK Krishna Menon, the then Defence Minister, to rectify regional and class imbalance amongst the officer cadre of the Indian Military.

Similar discrimination on grounds of gender prevails in Rashtriya Military Schools at Bangaluru, Belgaum (Karnataka), Ajmer, Dholpur (Rajasthan) and Chail (Himachal Pradesh), wherein admissions open to sons[2] of Defence Service Officers and civilians but not daughters.

The deprivation of quality education by denial of admission to girls in Sainik Schools and Rasthtriya Military Schools is against Constitutional guarantees of Articles 14, 15 and 21 A, and, hence, discriminatory. It is pertinent to mention that India loses around 1,600 military personnel every year without going to war, and the single biggest killers are said to be suicides; much more than counter-insurgency operations or firing

---

1   Now this condition is changed and even girls are allowed in Sainik Schools after the Hon'ble Supreme Court Order.

2   Now this condition has changed.

duels with Pakistan. Most importantly as reported soldiers undergo mental stress for not being able to take care of the problems being faced by their families back home.

What can be more worrying for a soldier than the education and security of his girl child, who is deprived of quality education? Further providing quality education to a daughter of a soldier is essential especially since the soldier is destined to spend most of his service life away from the family in service of the nation in some operational area or the other; including running the risk of not returning.

Chapter-1

Sainik Schools and Rashtriya Military Schools

Sainik Schools

Sainik Schools are fully residential schools run on public school lines. All the schools are members of All India Public Schools Conference. They offer a common curriculum and are affiliated to the CBSE, New Delhi. While developing a wholesome personality of the boys[1] so that they are fit for the NDA, the schools also prepare boys for class-X and XII examination of the CBSE as well as UPSC exam for the NDA.

The medium of instruction is English even though English is not a pre-requisite for admission. Since these schools prepare boys[2] for NDA in the +2 stage only the Science stream is offered. Besides academic excellence, the students are encouraged to develop creative faculties through co-curricular activities and socially useful work. They are systematically introduced to all major games and given compulsory NCC training upto class-XI. Adventure activities form an integral part of training. Each school has extensive infrastructure and land to cater to the needs of comprehensive training so that boys are brought up in conducive environment. Boys seeking admission in Class VI should be 10-11 yrs of age and for Class IX they should be aged 13-14 yrs as on 01 July in the year admission is being sought.

The **Sainik Schools** are a system of schools in India established and managed by the Sainik Schools Society under Ministry of Defence. They were conceived in 1961 by V. K. Krishna Menon, the then Defence Minister of India, to rectify the regional and class imbalance amongst the Officer

---

1   Now this condition is changed and even girls are allowed in Sainik Schools after the Hon'ble Supreme Court Order

2   Ibid

cadre of the Indian Military, and to prepare students for entry into the National Defence Academy (NDA), Khadakwasla, Pune and Indian Naval Academy. Today there are 26[3] such schools covering all the states of the country.

The schools are a brain child of Sh. V.K. Krishna Menon, the then Defence Minister. The other objectives of Sainik Schools are:-

a) To remove regional imbalance in the Officer cadre of the defence services.

b) To develop qualities of body, mind and character which will enable the young boys[4] to become good and useful citizens.

c) To bring Public School education within reach of the common man.

Sainik Schools offer a common curriculum and are affiliated to the CBSE, New Delhi. While developing a wholesome personality of the boys so that they are fit for the NDA, the schools also prepare boys for class-X and XII examination of the CBSE as well as UPSC exam for the NDA.

Rashtriya Military Schools

Rashtriya Military schools were established as King George's Royal Indian Military schools to take care of the education of the sons of defence personnel. In 1952, the schools were reorganized on Public School lines and admissions were made open to the sons of Defence Service Officers and civilians.

In 1954, the school became member of the Indian Public Schools Conference (IPSC) and continues to be an active member till date. The schools were renamed Military Schools in 1966 and its old motto, 'Play the Game' was replaced with 'Sheelem Param Bhushanam' which means Character is the Highest Virtue. On 25th Jun 2007, the schools got their present name "Rashtriya Military School".

The school has several of its alumni occupying high positions in the Armed Forces and in other sectors doing stellar service to the motherland. The schools are category 'A' establishment of the Army and are administrated by the Directorate General of Military Training at IHQ of MOD(Army).

---

3   Now there are 33 Sainik Schools across the country. Link: https://aissee.nta.nic.in/

4   Now this condition is changed and even girls are allowed in Sainik Schools after the Hon'ble Supreme Court Order

2

The Central Governing Council (CGC), headed by the Defence Secretary, Ministry of Defence is the apex body for these schools.

On the link of admission in the website i.e. http://www. rashtriyamilitaryschools.in/admission.html it is provided that Rashtriya Military Schools located at Bangalore, Belgaum (Karnataka) Ajmer, Dholpur (Rajasthan) and Chail (Himachal Pradesh). It is further provided that "Only boys[5] between 10 to 11 years of age for Class VI and Boys between 13 to 14 years of age for class IX of age as on 01 Jul of the academic year are eligible for admission. Six months relaxation in upper age limit is permissible for the wars of personnel killed in action."

Issue

Both the cases of not allowing girls/females candidates to be admitted to the Sainik Schools and Rashtriya Military Schools is a clear case of gender discrimination, in as much as males/boys candidates are admitted in both Sainik Schools and Rashtriya Military Schools but girls/females are denied admission. This denial of admission to girls/females in Sainik Schools and Rashtriya Military Schools is discriminatory and against the provision of Article 14 of the Constitution (Equality Before Law) which is a hallmark of our Constitution.

---

5   Now this condition is changed and even girls are allowed in Rashtriya Military Schools after the Hon'ble Supreme Court Order. Link: https://www.timesnownews.com/ education/rashtriya-military-schools-to-allow-admissions-to-girls-from-ay-2022-23-centre-informs-supreme-court-article-90089615

Chapter-2

Equality under Indian Constitution

Article 14 of the Indian Constitution talks about equality. It provides that State shall not deny to any person equality before law or the equal protection of laws within the territory of India.

Under Article 14 of the Constitution of India, every citizen has the right to equality of law and equal protection before law. The concept of an arbitrary action being in violation of Article 14 was first introduced in the case of *E.P. Royappa v. State of Tamil Nadu*, (1974) 4 SCC 3, wherein it was observed that 'equality is antithetic to arbitrariness'. Thus Article 14 has a very wide ambit and encompasses within it equality, the principles of natural justice and is a mandate against arbitrary state actions. This imposes a duty on the state to act fairly. Good governance in conformity with the mandate of Article 14, "raises a reasonable or legitimate expectation in every citizen to be treated fairly in its interaction with the state and its instrumentalities.[6]"

Because article 15 of the Indian Constitution talks about Prohibition of discrimination on grounds of religion, race, sex, caste or place of birth.

Article 39 A in Part IV of the Constitution deals with Directive Principles of State Policy which provides that the State shall direct its policies towards securing that the citizens, men and women equally, have the right to adequate means of livelihood. India adopted its Constitution in the year 1950 making provisions for Fundamental Rights to equality, freedom from exploitation, religion, cultural and educational rights of minorities and constitutional remedies. However, the right to free and compulsory elementary education was retained in Part-IV of the Constitution which incorporated the Directive Principles of State Policy. Article 45 as originally incorporated declared: The State shall endeavour to provide, within a period of 10 years from the commencement of the Constitution, for free

---

6 (Ref: Food Corporation of India. v. Kamdhenu Cattlefeed Industries Reported in (1993) 1 SCC 71)

and compulsory education for all children until they complete the age of 14 years.

Conferment of equal status on women apart from being a constitutional right has been recognized as a human right. In the words of Kofi Annan - "There is no tool more effective than the empowerment of women for development of a country."

Inequalities between the two sexes and discrimination against women have also been long-standing issues all over the world. Thus, women's pursuit of equality with man is a universal phenomenon.

Hon'ble Supreme Court in the case of **Charu Khurana vs Union of India,** AIR2015SC839 held that Equality cannot be achieved unless there are equal opportunities and if a woman is debarred at the threshold to enter into the sphere of a profession for which she is eligible and qualified, it is well-nigh impossible to conceive of equality. It also clips her capacity to earn her livelihood which affects her individual dignity.

For ready reference para 41 of is reproduced hereunder: "41. The aforesaid pronouncement clearly spells out that there cannot be any discrimination solely on the ground of gender. It is apt to note here that reservation of seats for women in panchayats and municipalities have been provided under Articles 243(d) and 243(t) of the Constitution of India. The purpose of the constitutional amendment is that the women in India are required to participate more in a democratic set-up especially at the grass root level. This is an affirmative step in the realm of women empowerment. The 73rd and 74th amendment of the Constitution which deal with the reservation of women has the avowed purpose, that is, the women should become parties in the decision making process in a democracy that is governed by rule of law. Their active participation in the decision making process has been accentuated upon and the secondary rule which was historically given to women has been sought to be metamorphosed to the primary one. The sustenance of gender justice is the cultivated achievement of intrinsic human rights. Equality cannot be achieved unless there are equal opportunities and if a woman is debarred at the threshold to enter into the sphere of profession for which she is eligible and qualified, it is well nigh impossible to conceive of equality. It also clips her capacity to earn her livelihood which affects her individual dignity."

In **Madhu Kishwar v. State of Bihar,** (1996) 5 SCC 125 Hon'ble Supreme Court had stated that Indian women have suffered and are suffering discrimination in silence.

In *Voluntary Health Assn. of Punjab v. Union of India,* (2013) 4 SCC 1, it has been observed by Court that it would not be an exaggeration to say that a society that does not respect its women cannot be treated to be civilised.

> When discrimination is sought to be made on the purported ground of classification and such classification must be founded on a rational criteria. The criteria which in absence of any constitutional provision and it will bear repetition to state, having regard to the societal conditions as they prevailed in the early 20th century, may not be rational criteria in the 21st century.

The socially ascribed roles of gender which are inherently discriminatory towards women should not form the backbone of taking any decision by the State. The state ought to exercise their control in a constitutionally justified manner.

Denial of entry in premier institutes run by the State is in violation of the Constitutional guarantee of equality as it denies women to avail extraordinary education and training opportunity as afforded to similarly placed men.

Chapter-3

Education and its Purpose

Bhartruhari in the 'Neethi Satakam' (First Century B.C.), emphasized the importance of education in the following words:

"Education is the special manifestation of man;

Education is the treasure which can be preserved without the fear of loss;

Education secures material pleasure, happiness and fame;

Education is the teacher of the teacher;

Education is God incarnate;

Education secures honour at the hands of the State, not money.

A man without education is equal to an animal."

Despite education being regarded as a pre-existing and natural right in every man and woman, it did not find a mention in the classic civil liberties instrument such as the English, Bill of Rights of 1689, the American Declaration of Independence of 1776 and the French Declaration of the Right of Man of 1789. However, the Rights of Man contained roots of the modern thought of inclusion - about equality, respect and decent education for all. The rise of socialism and liberalism in the 19th Century led nations to promote education as a matter of citizen's right and incorporate it in their Constitutions and legislations. The Constitution of the German Empire of 1849 had provisions relating to educational rights and the 1870 Education Act of England and Wales established a system of public education in the country. The Varsailles Treaty of 1919 was the first instance of international recognition of Right to Education to the Polish minorities as it is stated that 'they shall have an equal right to establish, manage and control at their own expense charitable, religious and social institutions, schools and other educational establishments. In the year 1924, the Declaration of Geneva under the auspice of the League of Nations recognized children's Right to Education by declaring that: 'The child must be given the means requisite for its normal development; the child that is backward must be helped and the child must be put in a position to earn its livelihood'. These principles later on, in the year 1959, formed the foundation of the Declaration of the Rights of Child, but before that in the year 1948, the Universal Declaration of Human Rights, recognizing education as a right, stated: Everyone has the right to education. Education shall be free, at least at the elementary and fundamental stage. Elementary education shall be compulsory. Technical and professional education shall be made generally available and higher education shall be equally accessible to all on the basis of merit [Article 26(1)]. Article 2 of the Universal Declaration characterized the non-discriminatory and equality-of-opportunity of the right to education by stating : 'everyone is entitled to all the rights..... without distinction of any kind, such as race, colour, sex, language, religion, political or other opinion, national or social origin, property, birth or other status.' Earl Warrren C.J. speaking for the U.S. Supreme Court in the decision reported as 347 US 483 (1954) *Brown v. Board of Education* observed: 'Today education is perhaps the most important function of State and local Governments. It is the very foundation of the good citizenship. Today it is the principal instrument in awakening the child to cultural values, in preparing him for later professional training, and in helping him to adjust normally to his environment. In these days, it is doubtful if any child may reasonably be expected to succeed in life if he is denied the opportunity of an education'. The right to education and equality of opportunity for access to it was asserted once again in the U.N. Convention on the Rights of the Child which was adopted by the U.N. General Assembly on November 29, 1989. Article 28(1) of the Convention states : 'States Parties recognise the right of the child to education, and with a view to achieving this right progressively and on the basis of equal opportunity, they shall, in particular : (a) make primary education compulsory and available free to all; (b) encourage the development of different forms of secondary education, including general and vocational education, make them available and accessible to every child, and appropriate measures such as the introduction of free and offering financial assistance in case of need; (c) make higher education accessible to all on the basis of capacity by every appropriate means.' The Salamanca Statement adopted following at the World Conference on Special Needs Education in Salamanca (Spain) in the year 1994 proclaimed that: 'regular schools with an inclusive orientation are the most effective means of combating discriminatory attitudes, creating welcoming communities, building an inclusive society and achieving education for all.'

At least two educational principles emerge from the series of U.N. Conventions : **(i) the right to free elementary education, and (ii) the right to equality of educational opportunity.**

Is there any inconsistency between the right to education and the compulsory nature of elementary education? The former gives a choice to exercise the right. The latter seems to impose compulsion on citizens. This seeming inconsistency is not real because compulsory elementary education is based on a notion that every person has an irrevocable entitlement to a period of education at public expense, implying therein that no person or body can prevent children from receiving basic education. This imposes an obligation on the State to ensure that children receive at least an elementary education in circumstances of parental neglect or ignorance.

In the Indian context, right to education developed during the freedom movement along with the demand for self-governance. In the year 1909 Gopal Krishna Gokhale introduced a Bill under the Indian Council Act of 1909, to make primary education compulsory and deserving of State funding. Regretfully, the Bill was defeated by a large majority. While addressing the legislature, Gokhale made the emotional observation that the issue would keep coming up again and again until all children realize their right to free and compulsory education. In 1937, at the National Education Conference held at Wardha, the Father of the Nation: Mahatma Gandhi used all the moral powers at his command to persuade the Ministers of Education of the newly elected Congress governments in seven provinces to give priority to basic education under Nai Taleem of seven years and allocate adequate funds for this purpose. The Ministers responded that there was no money, in spite thereof, the Wardha Conference passed four resolutions, the first amongst which stated : Free and compulsory education be provided for seven years on a nation-wide scale. This resolution was re-iterated at the 51st annual session of the Indian National Congress held at Haripura in February 1938.

Purpose of Education

"Life is but a wintry day;

Some come to breakfast and away;

Other to dinner stay

And are full fed;

The Oldest man but sups

And goes to bed"

Education is the most potent mechanism for the advancement of human beings. It enlarges, enriches and improves an individual's image of the future. It emancipates the human beings and leads to liberation from ignorance. A man without education is no more than an animal. It is said that in the twenty-first century, 'a nation's ability to convert knowledge into wealth and social good through the process of innovation is going to determine its future,' accordingly twenty-first century is termed as century of knowledge. Educational institutions are those sacred places where the youth acquire knowledge and wisdom; who in turn determine the future of a nation. It is the number of educational institutions and their quality, which to a great extent, determine the progress of a nation. The educational institutions collectively work as the backbone of a developed nation. Every educational institution has to maintain certain standard of education. It is this standard which determines the level of prosperity, welfare and security of people. It is also interlinked with the development of nation in general. Education is now charged with responsibility for what is referred to as 'human capital formation' or 'human resource development'. This task is guided by the assumption that in every society there is a limited pool of individuals with a high level of intelligence, spread across all sectors of society. These talented individuals have to be selected and equipped with knowledge and skills, and promoted to run the engines of industrial growth. Others have to be suitably educated to serve as white-collar or blue-collar workers and supervisors. In the context of the doctrine of economic nationalism, it is believed that the prosperity of a nation depends on how well its system of education performs this task.[7] While educational institutions providing elementary education aim at ensuring higher literacy rate by providing access to all, institutions providing higher education aim at producing more and more expert professionals and scholars who can serve the nation and its people in a better way. Therefore, it is to be ensured that there must be quality higher education so that the nation produces the best professionals and scholars. Any step, big or small, compromising with the quality of education can't be accepted in the long run.

The multiplication of universities and colleges has hardly kept pace with

---

7   Suma Chitnis, "Higher Education", in Veena Das (ed.), *The Oxford India Companion to Sociology and Social Anthropology* 1050 (Oxford University Press, London, 2003).

the insatiable needs of the world's most populous democracy. By and large, our education system has not been adequate for the task of turning out a sufficient number of young leaders who can lift the country out of the polluted waters of our public life and the slime and sludge of a corrupted economy.

The most important function of education- enriching the character. What we need today more than anything else is moral leadership- founded on courage, intellectual integrity and a sense of values. The objective of higher education should be to turn our integrated personalities in whom have been inculcated noble ideas. On the University campus we must stress the importance of Individual self-fulfillment but not self-indulgence, group cohesiveness but not group jingoism, work and achievement but not power and acquisitiveness for their own sake. A university campus is the one place where the virtues of discipline and non-violence should be written as with a sunbeam on every student's mind.   Your education has been in vain if it has not fostered in you the habit of clear, independent thinking. There are well-dressed foolish ideas, just as there are well-dressed fools, and the discerning man must be able to recognize them as such. As Bertrand Russell Observed, "There is no nonsense so arrant that it cannot be made the creed of the vast majority by adequate governmental action. Man is a credulous animal and must believe something; in the absence of good grounds for belief, he will be satisfied with bad ones." Without clarity of though and readiness to admit our mistakes, it would be impossible to solve our economic problems. "A Man," said Lin Yutang, "who has an uncleared stomach spends all his thoughts on his stomach, so a society with a sick and aching economy is forever pre-occupied with thoughts of economies." If eager boys and girls are not to be thrown on the scrap-heap of the unemployed, it is imperative that we stop our ideological incursions into the higher forms of irrationality. If we cannot have economic policies that make for plenty, let us at least have policies that make sense. It is important that citizens must obey the law. It is even more important that citizens must obey the high standards of decency which are not enforced by the law but are the hallmark of a truly civilized and mature democracy. Sir Thomas Taylor of Aberdeen University summed up the position in a few memorable sentences. As he put it, beyond the sphere of duty which is legally enforceable, there is a vast range of significant behaviour in which the law does not and ought not to intervene. This feeling of obedience to the unenforceable is the very opposite of the attitude that whatever is technically possible is allowable. This power of self-discipline is the very opposite of the fatal arrogance, which asserts, whether in government,

11

science, industry or personal behaviour, that whatever is technically possible is licit. All through history, men have needed it to preserve them from the temper which hardens the heart and perverts the understanding.

It is essential that the student during education acquire an understanding of and a lively feeling for values. He must acquire a vivid sense of the beautiful and of the normally good. Otherwise he- with his specialized knowledge- more closely resembles a well-trained dog than a harmoniously developed person.

Professor Walter Raleigh said that the college final and day of Judgment are two different examinations. Failures may also take some consolation from the fact that A.E. Housman, the great scholar of Greek and Latin, and better known as poet, once failed in the papers on those very languages at the Oxford University. His Biographer Richards comments, "The Nightangle got no prize at the Poultry Show". Even Rabindranath Tagore (Poet from India) was an utter failure in school but a legendary poet. In ancient India, kings and emperors thought it a privilege to sit at the feet of a man of learning. Intellectuals and men of knowledge were given the highest honour in society. King Janaka, himself a philosopher, journeyed on foot into the jungle to discourse with yajnavalkya on high matters of state. In the eighth century Sankaracharya travelled on foot from Kerala to Kashmir and from Dwarka in the west to Puri in the east. He could not have changed men's minds and established centres of learning in the far-flung corners of India but for the great esteem and reverence which intellectuals enjoyed.

Unfortunately, in our times we have down-graded the intellectual and have devalued the very word. Today an "intellectual" means a man who is intelligent enough to know on which side his bread is buttered. It has been said that there are two kinds of fools in the world—those who give advice and those who do not take it. Education has been called the technique of transmitting civilization. In order that it may transmit civilization, it has to perform two major functions: it must enlighten the understanding, and it must enrich the character. The two marks of a truly educated man, whose understanding has been enlightened, are the capacity to think clearly and intellectual curiosity.

In the eighteenth century, Dean Swift said that the majority of men were as fit for flying as for thinking. Technology has made it possible for men to fly, or at least to sit in a contraption that flies, but it has not made it possible for men to think. If your education has made it possible for you to think for yourself on the problems which face you and which face the country, your college has done very well by you. If this habit of thinking for yourself has not been inculcated in you, you would be well advised to acquire it after you leave college.

As the cynic remarked, a formal education at a university cannot do you much harm provided you start learning thereafter. The capacity to think clearly should enable the student to sift, and reject when necessary, the ideas and ideologies which are perpetually inflicted on him by the mass media of communication. It should enable him to realize that these mass media are in chains, - in chains to the foolish and narrowing purposes of selling consumer goods, and to the narrowing and stifling purposes of politics. A liberal education is prophylactic against unthinking acceptance of the modern "mantras[8]" which are kept in current circulation by the mass media. If we continue to force children to memorize the dates of wars without asking why we have perpetual war; if we continue to force children to memorize mathematical precepts without understanding how and why we use math; if we continue to force children to learn to read while ignoring literacy, we should not expect anything different than what we have had for many years: a bewildered herd. If, however, we want something much different for our children, for our communities, and indeed for the world, then we must take a radically different approach to how we educate future citizens.

The education system in our country is also facing a challenge of lack of excellence. The pace of economic growth in the country and opportunities present can only be availed if human resources development in the country is adequate. There is a need for improvement in the quality of education and training. The NASSCOM –Mackinsey Report (2005) had said that not more than 15 % of graduates of general education and 25-30 % of technical education are fit for employment. This was a shocking revelation. The writing on the wall was clear that Indian education system must strive for excellence. On the one hand there needs to be improvement in higher education facilities in the country. On the other hand, there is need of improvement in school and undergraduate education. School curriculum needs to be oriented to be more specialized. It should be flexible according to the needs of student's aptitude and interest. So students can opt for the field of interest early. Also, those with academic and research interests can get appropriate guidance. Teaching methods also needs adopt modern techniques like use of multimedia and equipments. Pratham has came

---

8   Expressions or formulate meant to be recited and supposed to have occult effect.

out with new teaching methods for children which makes learning a fun. Knowledge of computers as part of education and rainig is indispensible for anyone. Vocational training alongside education can help to provide practical knowledge. Incentives for improving quality of education should be provided to both government and private institutions. Also industries and corporates must come forward to train the human resources. It is jokingly said about the Roman Civilization, that they excelled in drains but not in brains. The reason being that they gave many engineering feats but made no achievement in science. So in our efforts of providing market needed human resources we need not to forget the importance of basic research and fundamental knowledge. Also Sports and Arts are the field which have great prospects; their improvement should not be forgotten. State of art stadiums, gymnasiums, courts, swimming pool, etc needs to be constructed widely so talented sportsperson can come forward. There is a great deal of work done to improve the condition of study of humanities and arts so as to promote research and innovation in one hand and conservation of traditional knowledge on the other. In spite of many efforts, the education system in India is still not fully inclusive. There are many sections of society who are out of the system due to different reasons. All our efforts will go in vain if there remains in our country few pockets of illiteracy. Inclusion is a tough challenge as it is linked to our society's social and traditional factors. That's why its solution also lies in wider social interventions.

If we want democracy, we must educate for democracy. Democracy is a form of associated living that fosters the growth of the individual through her participation in social affairs. Free, reflective, critical inquiry and the welfare of others undergird interaction, communion, and community building. Unlike authoritarian modes of government, democracy requires its members to participate in the political, social, cultural, and economic institutions affecting their development and, unlike authoritarian countries, democracies believe in the capacity of ordinary individuals to direct the affairs of their communities, especially their schools.

The trajectory our schools now follow does not bode well for democracy. The No Child Left Behind Act produces a hyper-productive, blindly obedient, worksheet completing citizenry, one capable of voting for American Idols, but one unable to recognize larger threats to humanity. The country must develop education for democratic participation, a type of education that helps children mature into intelligent, critical, engaged, reflective, and compassionate members of their schools and communities.

Active participation in institutions prevents authoritarianism and allows for individual and community re-creation and growth. Privatizing or standardizing institutions does quite the opposite.

Democracy is about majority rule by an educated and well informed citizenry, thus democracy is dependant upon a civic press that monitors the health of our democracy. Democracy is about the common good, the dignity and human worth of every citizen. It is about We the People and the higher angels of our nature. Again, it is about spirituality. Education is firmly in control by the State. It should be no surprise that the State uses this power to propagate its needs. Education will never be truly reformed until the State loses power over it. Education must be controlled by the people.

All the troubles may be summed up in three lines (T.S. Eliot)

> *"where is the Life we have lost in living?*
>
> *Where is the wisdom we have lost in Knowledge?*
>
> *Where is the knowledge we have lost in information?"*

Chapter-4

Right to Education

The Fundamental Rights in the Constitution of India are close to the U.N.'s Universal Declaration on Human Rights with the most important fundamental right, impacting on the life of the people in India, being Article 21, which guarantees 'right to life and personal liberty'. It declares: 'No person shall be deprived of his life or personal liberty except according to procedure established by law'. This right is akin to the French concept of Right of Man, which draws from the principal that the people's life chances should not be restricted by irrelevant considerations. Education is key to assuring 'people's life chances'.

Article 21 of the Constitution of India has been interpreted and reinterpreted 'n' number of times by the Supreme Court of India and its horizon has been constantly expanded keeping in view the march of times. From the point of view of education, the landmark decision would be the Constitution Bench judgment of the Supreme Court reported as *Unni Krishnan, J.P. & Ors. v. State of A.P. & Ors.,* (1993) 1 SCC 645 Holding that the provisions of Parts-III and IV of the Constitution of India are supplementary and complimentary to each other and that fundamental rights are but a means to achieve the goal indicated in Part-IV, the Supreme Court held that the fundamental rights must be construed in the light of the directive principles.

The logical corollary of the decision of the Supreme Court in Unni Krishnan case would be that free elementary education is an essential sovereign function of the welfare state because education is a cardinal component of human dignity. It took time for the legislature to respond, but the response came when Article 21A was inserted in Part III of the Constitution of India by the Constitution (86th Amendment) Act, 2000. Article 21A of the Constitution of India reads: 'The State shall provide free and compulsory education to all children of the age of six to fourteen years in such manner as the State may, by law, determine.' The Preamble to the Constitution of

India evinces that, amongst others, one essential sovereign duty of the State is to secure 'equality of status and opportunity and assuring the dignity of the individual.'

The Constitution (Eighty-sixth Amendment) Act, 2002 inserted Article 21-A in the Constitution of India to provide free and compulsory education of all children in the age group of six to fourteen years as a Fundamental Right in such a manner as the State may, by law, determine. The Right of Children to Free and Compulsory Education (RTE) Act, 2009, which represents the consequential legislation envisaged under Article 21-A, means that every child has a right to full time elementary education of satisfactory and equitable quality in a formal school which satisfies certain essential norms and standards. 'Compulsory education' casts an obligation on the appropriate Government and local authorities to provide and ensure admission, attendance and completion of elementary education by all children in the **6-14** age group. With this, India has moved forward to a rights-based framework that casts a legal obligation on the Central and State Governments to implement this fundamental child right as enshrined in the Article 21A of the Constitution, in accordance with the provisions of the RTE Act.

Notable is the fact that Education is one of the most critical areas of empowerment for women, and Sainik Schools and Rashtriya Military Schools, both illustrate clear examples of discrimination girls/women suffer. Offering girls basic quality education is one sure way of giving them much greater power, of enabling them to make genuine choices over the kinds of lives they wish to lead. By denial of daughters of soldiers/defence personnel the basic right to quality education, the Sainik Schools and Rashtriya Military Schools are perpetrating gender inequalities.

Education is one of the most critical areas of empowerment for women, and Sainik Schools and Rashtriya Military Schools, both illustrate clear examples of discrimination girls/women suffer. Offering girls basic quality education is one sure way of giving them much greater power, of enabling them to make genuine choices over the kinds of lives they wish to lead. India having ratified The Convention on the Rights of the Child and the Convention on the Elimination of All Forms of Discrimination against Women; and as guaranteed by Article 21 A of the Constitution of India, all establish education as a basic human right.

Articles 14, 15 and 16 of the Constitution guarantee non-discrimination and equality before law. The Preamble of the Constitution gives the direction in which the State must move i.e. to secure to all its citizens equality of status. Thus the principle of equality is strongly expressed in the Constitution and is also in consonance with the commitments made by India by virtue of being a party to a number of international instruments.

Education is the foundation on which the society seeks to build its edifice of social harmony. It is the means through which one hopes to root out the divides that exists in society and integrate the country. Various commissions have highlighted that the current multilayered school system, be it in India or abroad, promotes and maintains the wide chasm that exists between the advantaged and disadvantaged. The privilege, who can afford to buy education, have access to the high-quality elite schools, while the poor and the marginalized are left to wallow in ill-equipped schools established by the municipalities, gram panchayats and Government. Many perceive that education has become a commodity. They believe that the system is inherently flawed, in that, the very means through which an egalitarian society is sought to be built is tailored in such a manner that it becomes a seat of, and a cause for, naturalising and legitimizing decisiveness and social segregation.

The deprivation of quality education by denial of admission to girls/ females in Sainik Schools and Rasthtriya Military Schools is against Constitutional guarantees of Article 14,15 and 21 A, hence discriminatory. It is pertinent to mention that India loses around 1,600 military personnel every year without going to war, and one the single biggest killers are said to be suicides; much more than counter-insurgency operations or firing duels with Pakistan. Most importantly as reported soldiers undergo mental stress for not being able to take care of the problems being faced by their families back home.

Crucial role of universal elementary education for strengthening the social fabric of democracy

The Statement of Objects and Reasons of the Right of Children to Free and Compulsory Education Act, 2009[9] (hereinafter referred to as the 'RTE Act') recognises one of the most profound underlying principle contained in the Constitution, viz. the crucial role of universal elementary education for

---

9   The **Right of Children to Free and Compulsory Education Act** or **Right to Education Act (RTE)** is an Act of the Parliament of India enacted on 4 August 2009, which describes the modalities of the importance of free and compulsory education for children between the age of 6 to 14 years in India under Article 21A of the Indian Constitution.

strengthening the social fabric of democracy through provision of equal opportunities to all has been accepted, since inception of our Republic. Other, and equally significant principle that it recognises, is that, in order to ensure equal opportunities to all citizens, it is necessary that elementary education is provided to one and all. Keeping in view this spirit, obligation was imposed upon the State, as per Article 41[10], read with Article 45[11], of the Constitution to make effective provisions for securing the right to education, among other. Thus, it is one of the Directive Principles of State Policy[12] enumerated in the Constitution that the State shall provide free and compulsory education to all children. In order to make it a reality, Supreme Court in the case of Unni Krishnan, J.P. and Ors. v. State of Andhra Pradesh and Ors., (1993) 1 SCC 645 stretched the limits of Article 45 by reading right to free education as a fundamental right[13] of children upto the age of 14 years so as to enable the children up to the age of 14 years to receive the education as a matter of right. Law Commission also supported it by making recommendation[14] to the Parliament to make suitable amendment in the Constitution. Realising its constitutional commitment,

---

10 **Article 41 in The Constitution Of India 1949**
    41. Right to work, to education and to public assistance in certain cases The State shall, within the limits of its economic capacity and development, make effective provision for securing the right to work, to education and to public assistance in cases of unemployment, old age, sickness and disablement, and in other cases of undeserved want

11 **Article 41 in The Constitution Of India 1949**
    41. Right to work, to education and to public assistance in certain cases The State shall, within the limits of its economic capacity and development, make effective provision for securing the right to work, to education and to public assistance in cases of unemployment, old age, sickness and disablement, and in other cases of undeserved want

12 The **Directive Principles of State Policy** (DPSP) are the guidelines or principles given to the federal institutes governing the state of **India**, to be kept in citation while framing laws and policies. These provisions, contained in Part IV (Article 36–51) of the Constitution of India, are not enforceable by any court, but the principles laid down there in are not considered in the governance of the country, making it the duty of the State to apply these principles in making laws to establish a just society in the country.

13 **Fundamental rights**, the basic and civil liberties of the people, are protected under the charter of rights contained in Part III (Articles 12 to 35) of the Constitution of India. These include individual rights common to most liberal democracies, such as equality before the law, freedom of speech and expression, religious and cultural freedom, peaceful assembly, freedom to practice religion, and the right to constitutional remedies for the protection of civil rights by means of writs such as Habeas Corpus, Mandamus, Prohibition, Certiorari and Quo Warranto.

14 Report No. 165 of the Law Commission of India

the Parliament obliged, and Article 21-A[15] was added vide the Constitution (Eighty Sixth Amendment) Act, 2002 in the following manner:

Article 21-A. Right to education.-The State shall provide free and compulsory education to all children of the age of six to fourteen years in such manner as the State may, by law, determine.

Simultaneously, Article 45 of the Constitution was also substituted with the following Article:

Article 45. Provision for early childhood care and education to children below the age of six years.-The State shall endeavour to provide early childhood care and education for all children until they complete the age of six years.

Notwithstanding the aforesaid provisions in the Constitution and significant spatial and numerical expansion of elementary schools in the country, it was found that number of children, particularly children from disadvantaged groups and weaker sections, who drop out of school before completing elementary education, remains very large. It was also noticed that the quality of learning achievement is not always entirely satisfactory even in the case of children who complete elementary education. Having regard to the aforesaid harsh realities, the Parliament enacted the RTE Act with the following objects in mind:

(a) that every child has a right to be provided full-time elementary education of satisfactory and equitable quality in a formal school which satisfies certain essential norms and standards;

(b) 'compulsory education' casts an obligation on the appropriate Government to provide and ensure admission, attendance and completion of elementary education;

(c) 'free education' means that no child, other than a child who has been admitted by his or her parents to a school which is not supported by the appropriate Government, shall be liable to pay any kind of fee or charges or expenses which may prevent him or her from pursuing and completing elementary education;

(d) the duties and responsibilities of the appropriate Government, local authorities, parents, schools and teachers in providing free

---

15 Chapter 1: Preliminary notes on transformative constitutionalism from Transformative Constitutionalism: Comparing the apex courts of Brazil, India and South Africa: by Oscar Vilhena, Upendra Baxi and Frans Viljoen (editors); South Asian Edition 2014

and compulsory education; and

(e) a system for the protection of the right of children and a decentralized grievance redressal mechanism.

It hardly needs to be emphasized that for turning the provision of every child to have free and compulsory education into reality, not only sufficient number of schools are required with all necessary facilities and infrastructure, adequate and qualified teaching staff shall also be needed to fulfill this noble purpose.

A Constitution Bench[16] of Supreme Court in M. Nagaraj and Ors. v. Union of India and Ors., (2006) 8 SCC 212 felt it necessary to make following remarks:

> *Equality of opportunity has two different and distinct concepts. There is a conceptual distinction between a non-discrimination principle and affirmative action under which the State is obliged to provide a level-playing field to the oppressed classes. Affirmative action in the above sense seeks to move beyond the concept of non-discrimination towards equalising results with respect to various groups. Both the conceptions constitute "equality of opportunity".*

Going by the scheme of the Constitution, it is more than obvious that the framers had kept in mind social and economic conditions of the marginalised Section of the society, and in particular, those who were backward and discriminated against for centuries. Chapters on 'Fundamental Rights' as well as 'Directive Principles of State Policies' eloquently bear out the challenges of overcoming poverty, discrimination and inequality, promoting equal access to group quality education, health and housing, untouchability and exploitation of weaker section. In making such provisions with a purpose of eradicating the aforesaid ills with which marginalized Section of Indian society was suffering (in fact, even now continue to suffer in great measure), we, the people gave us the Constitution which is transformative in nature. Vision depicted therein was to aim at achieving agaratarian society. Professor Upendra Baxi brings out this transformative feature of the Indian Constitution, so brilliantly in the following words:

---

16 **Constitution bench** is the name given to the benches of the Supreme Court of India which consist of at least five judges of the court which sit to decide any case "involving a substantial question of law as to the interpretation" of the Constitution of India or "for the purpose of hearing any reference" made by the President of India under Article 143.

To be sure, the Indian Constitution frontally addresses millennial wrongs such as untouchability; indeed, the constitution is transformative on this normative register. It is historically the first modern constitution not merely to declare constitutionally unlawful the practice of discrimination on the 'grounds of untouchability' (Article 23[17] and 24[18]). A unique feature of these provisions consists in the creation of constitutional offence, even to the point of derogation of the design and detail of Indian federalism, because Article 35 empowers a parliamentary override over the legislative of the states within the Indian union. How many we understand in the Indian case the differential reconstitutions of memories of ancient wrongs as providing the very leitmotif of constitutional change compared with the organization of collective amnesia concerning the Partition Holocaust? Does this question to all matter in any understanding of Indian Constitution now at work?

True, transformative constitutionals texts and contexts remain the very last sites for language of love, gift, belonging and care.[19] Professor Baxi identifies three 'C's of constitutionalism[20]. C1 is the text of Constitution,

---

17 **Article 23 in The Constitution Of India 1949**
    23. Prohibition of traffic in human beings and forced labour
    (1) Traffic in human beings and begar and other similar forms of forced labour are prohibited and any contravention of this provision shall be an offence punishable in accordance with law
    (2) Nothing in this article shall prevent the State from imposing compulsory service for public purpose, and in imposing such service the State shall not make any discrimination on grounds only of religion, race, caste or class or any of them

18 **Article 24 in The Constitution Of India 1949**
    24. Prohibition of employment of children in factories, etc No child below the age of fourteen years shall be employed to work in any factory or mine or engaged in any other hazardous employment Provided that nothing in this sub clause shall authorise the detention of any person beyond the maximum period prescribed by any law made by Parliament under sub clause (b) of clause (7); or such person is detained in accordance with the provisions of any law made by Parliament under sub clauses (a) and (b) of clause (7)

19 Chapter 1: Preliminary notes on transformative constitutionalism from Transformative Constitutionalism: Comparing the apex courts of Brazil, India and South Africa: by Oscar Vilhena, Upendra Baxi and Frans Viljoen (editors); South Asian Edition 2014

20 Though in the aforesaid Chapter, he has expanded it to 8 'C's, other 'C's are different facets to C2. He elaborates these 'C's as under.
    "Understanding the 'transformative' in BISA and related comparative constitutional studies (COSOG) contexts entails further division of C2 beyond the official (of authoritative) interpretation by others. Via. C4, I designate practices of non official interpretation from the learned professions, including public intellectuals and social and human rights movements. CS designates all persons in a dominant position- 'corporate'

C2 is the constitutional law which is the official interpretation (namely, the way it is interpreted by the courts) and C3, in the conventional sense invites attention to the normative theory or ideological core or even the 'spirit of constitutions'. The task of transformating the constitutionalism is primarily that of the Courts, particularly the Apex Court, while enforcing the provisions of the Constitution. It is for this reason that Supreme Court has always interpret the text of the Constitution in such a way that 'spirit' of the constitution is realised.

When our Constitution envisages equal respect and concern for each individual in the society and the attainment of the goal requires special attention to be paid to some, that ought to be done. Giving of desired concessions to the reserved category persons, thus, ensures equality as a levelling process. At jurisprudential level, whether reservation policies are defended on compensatory principles, utilitarian principles or on the principle of distributive justice, fact remains that the very ethos of such policies is to bring out equality, by taking affirmative action. Indian Constitution has made adequate enabling provisions empowering the State to provide such concessions.

'financial', 'market' and 'consumer' citizens-who especially contest C2 to advance their own strategic interest. C6 comprises interpretive praxes emanating from the voice of human and social suffering of the rightless or the worst-off citizens and persons who claims the human 'right to have rights [This is a favorite notion of Hannah Arendt. See, for a recent analysis, W. Hamacher 'The right to have a rights (four-and-a half remarks)' (2004) 103 South Atlantic Quarterly 343. See also FI michelman 'Parsing a "right to have rights" '(1996) 3 Constellations 200.] C6 often stands articulated by communities of resistance-for short here, on the power of social movements and human rights struggles. For C6 interpretive praxes to have any substantive impact on constitutional law (C2) the hospitable figuration of activists justices remains necessary; perhaps, this is best named as a distinctive C7.

At the same time, we also need to consider C8- the constituted powers to suspend constitutions in the state of within-notion emergency often named as ' armed rebellion', or external threats most poignantly manifest in the contemporary grammars and rhetoric of 'wars on terror'.

Chapter-5

Private unaided schools autonomy to admit students[21]

Question before the High Court

The primary legal issue that arises for consideration in the writ petitions[22]

---

21 Appellants: **Forum For Promotion of Quality Education For All Vs.** Respondent: **Lt. Governor of Delhi AND** Appellants: **Action Committee unaided Recognized Private Schools Vs.** Respondent: **Hon'ble Lt. Governor**
2014(146)DRJ462, W.P. (C) 202 and 177/2014, Decided On: 28.11.2014
Hon'ble Judges/Coram: Manmohan, Judge, High Court of Delhi
Subject: Constitution of India

22 **Meaning of Writ Petition:**
A petition seeking issuance of a writ is a writ petition. Pits in the first instance in the High Courts and the Supreme Court are writ petitions.
A writ of habeas corpus is issued to an authority or person to produce in court a person who is either missing or kept in illegal custody. Where the detention is found to be without authority of law, the Court may order compensation to the person illegally detained.
A writ of mandamus is a direction to an authority to either do or refrain from doing a particular act. For instance, a writ to the Pollution Control Board to strictly enforce the Pollution Control Acts. For a mandamus to be issued, it must be shown:
a) That the authority was under obligation, statutory or otherwise to act in a particular manner;
b) that the said authority failed in performing such obligation;
c) that such failure has resulted in some specific violation of a fundamental right of either the petitioner or an indeterminate class of persons.
A writ of certiorari is a direction to an authority to produce before the Court the records on the basis of which a decision under challenge in the writ petition has been taken. By looking into those records, the Court will examine whether the authority applied its mind to the relevant materials before it took the decision. If the Court finds that no reasonable person could come to the decision in question, it will set aside (quash) that decision and give a further direction to the authority to consider the matter afresh.For instance, the permission given by an authority to operate a distillery next to a school can be challenged by filing a petition asking for a writ of certiorari.
A writ of prohibition issues to prevent a judicial authority subordinate to the High

24

was whether private unaided schools have the authority to admit students and the children through their parents have a right to choose a school in which they wish to study or whether the executive by way of an office order can impose a formula on the basis of which nursery admissions have to be carried out by such schools.

Facts in Nutshell

Writ petitions were filed by a committee and a forum representing private unaided recognized schools challenging office orders dated 18th December, 2013 and 27th December, 2013 issued by Lieutenant Governor of Delhi amending Clause 14 of the earlier notifications pertaining to nursery admissions on the ground amongst others that they are illegal, arbitrary and without jurisdiction. By the impugned office orders, the Lieutenant Governor has directed that seventy-five per cent nursery students, i.e., after excluding twenty-five per cent seats reserved for economically weaker section, shall be admitted on the following basis:-

- 70 marks for neighbourhood;

- 20 marks for siblings;

- 5 marks for parent/alumni; and

- 5 marks for inter-state transfers.

By a subsequent circular, five marks for inter-state transfers were withdrawn and the controversy with regard to the same has been put to rest by the judgment dated 7th May, 2014 passed by the Apex Court.

Court from exercising jurisdiction over a matter pending before it. This could be on the ground that the authority lacks jurisdiction and further that prejudice would be caused if the authority proceeds to decide the matter. Where the authority is found to be biased and refuses to rescue, a writ of prohibition may issue.

A petition seeking a writ of quo warranto questions the legal basis and authority of a person appointed to public office. For instance, the appointment of a member of a Public Service Commission not qualified to hold the post can be questioned by a writ of quo warranto and appointment nullified if found to be illegal.

A writ of declaration issues to declare an executive, legislative or quasi- judicial act to be invalid in law. For instance, a court could declare S. 81 of the Mental Health Act, 1987 that permits use of mentally ill patients for experimentation to be violative of the fundamental rights of the mentally ill and therefore illegal and void. A petition seeking such declaratory relief must also necessarily seek certain consequential reliefs. For instance, immediate discontinuance of the illegal practice and appropriate remedial compensation.

Right to Education:

Right to education of Children between the age of three and six years is a fundamental right[23] under Articles 21[24] and 45[25] of the Constitution and the State is bound to ensure that the said right is available to all children, particularly in the light of Sections 11 and 35 of the RTE Act, 2009. The said Sections are reproduced hereinbelow:-

"11. Appropriate Government to provide for preschool education-With a view to prepare children above the age of three years for elementary education and to provide early childhood care and education for all children until they complete the age of six years, the appropriate government may make necessary arrangement for providing free pre-school education for such children

XXXX XXXX XXXX XXXX

35.(1) The Central Government may issue such guidelines to the appropriate Government or, as the case may be, the local authority, as it deems fit for the purposes of implementation of the provisions of this Act.

(2) The appropriate Government may issue guidelines and give such directions, as it deems fit, to the local authority or the School Management

---

23 **Fundamental rights** is a charter of rights contained in the Constitution of India. It guarantees civil liberties such that all Indians can lead their lives in peace and harmony as citizens of India. These include individual rights common to most liberal democracies, such as equality before law, freedom of speech and expression, and peaceful assembly, freedom to practice religion, and the right to constitutional remedies for the protection of civil rights by means of writs such as habeas corpus. Violation of these rights result in punishments as prescribed in the Indian Penal Code or other special laws, subject to discretion of the judiciary. The Fundamental Rights are defined as basic human freedoms which every Indian citizen has the right to enjoy for a proper and harmonious development of personality. These rights universally apply to all citizens, irrespective of race, place of birth, religion, caste or gender. Aliens (persons who are not citizens) are also considered in matters like equality before law. They are enforceable by the courts, subject to certain restrictions. The Rights have their origins in many sources, includingEngland's Bill of Rights, the United States Bill of Rights and France's Declaration of the Rights of Man.

24 **Article 21 in The Constitution Of India 1949**

21. Protection of life and personal liberty No person shall be deprived of his life or personal liberty except according to procedure established by law

25 **Article 45 in The Constitution Of India 1949**

45. Provision for free and compulsory education for children The State shall endeavour to provide, within a period of ten years from the commencement of this Constitution, for free and compulsory education for all children until they complete the age of fourteen years

Committee regarding the implementation of the provisions of this Act.

(3) The local authority may issue guidelines and give such directions, as it deems fit, to the School Management Committee regarding implementation of the provisions of this Act."

Private Unaided school management have a fundamental right under Articles 19(1)(g) to establish run and administer their schools, including the right to admit students:

In *T.M.A. Pai Foundation and Others vs. State of Karnataka and Others*[26], the eleven judge Bench has held that the establishment and running of an educational institution falls within the four expressions used in Article 19(1)(g)[27] of the Constitution, in particular the expression "occupation".

The right to admit students amongst others was held by the Supreme Court in T.M.A. Pai Foundation (supra) to be a facet of the right to establish and administer schools, conferred upon private unaided non-minority educational institutions. The Supreme Court held that conferring maximum autonomy upon private unaided schools would be in the interest of general public as it would ensure that more such institutions are established.

The importance of schools has been aptly expressed by Victor Hugo when he said, "He who opens a School door, closes a prison." James A. Garfield has also wisely said, "Next in importance to freedom and justice is popular education, without which neither freedom nor justice can be permanently maintained."

The relevant portion of T.M.A. Pai Foundation (supra) is reproduced hereinbelow:-

"Article 19(1)(g) employs four expressions, viz., profession, occupation, trade and business. Their fields may overlap, but each of them does have a content

---

26 (2002) 8 SCC 481

27 **Article 19 in The Constitution Of India 1949**
  19. Protection of certain rights regarding freedom of speech etc
  (1) All citizens shall have the right
  (a) to freedom of speech and expression;
  (b) to assemble peaceably and without arms;
  (c) to form associations or unions;
  (d) to move freely throughout the territory of India;
  (e) to reside and settle in any part of the territory of India; and
  (f) omitted
  (g) to practise any profession, or to carry on any occupation, trade or business

of its own. Education is per se regarded as an activity that is charitable in nature[See The State of Bombay v. R.M.D. Chamarbaugwala,. Education has so far not been regarded as a trade or business where profit is the motive. Even if there is any doubt about whether education is a profession or not, it does appear that education will fall within the meaning of the expression "occupation".

The establishment and running of an educational institution where a large number of persons are employed as teachers or administrative staff, and an activity is carried on that results in the imparting of knowledge to the students, must necessarily be regarded as an occupation, even if there is no element of profit generation. It is difficult to comprehend that education, per se, will not fall under any of the four expressions in Article 19(1)(g).

Private unaided non-minority educational institutions:

Private education is one of the most dynamic and fastest growing segments of post-secondary education at the turn of the twenty-first century.

The right to establish and administer broadly comprises the following rights:-

    (a) to admit students

    (b) to set up a reasonable fee structure

    (c) to constitute a governing body;

    (d) to appoint staff (teaching and non-teaching); and

    (e) to take action if there is dereliction of duty on the part of any

But the essence of a private educational institution is the autonomy that the institution must have in its management and administration. There, necessarily, has to be a difference in the administration of private unaided institutions and the government-aided institutions. Whereas in the latter case, the Government will have greater say in the administration, including admissions and fixing of fees, in the case of private unaided institutions, maximum autonomy in the day-to-day administration has to be with the private unaided institutions. Bureaucratic or governmental interference in the administration of such an institution will undermine its independence. While an educational institution is not a business, in order to examine the degree of independence that can be given to a recognized educational institution, like any private entity that does not seek aid or assistance from the Government, and that exists by virtue of the funds generated by it, including its loans or borrowings, it is important to note that the essential ingredients of the management of the private institution include the recruiting students and staff, and the quantum of fee that is to be charged.

Education is taught at different levels, from primary to professional. It is, therefore, obvious that government regulations for all levels or types of educational institutions cannot be identical; so also, the extent of control or regulation could be greater vis-à-vis aided institutions.

In the case of unaided private schools, maximum autonomy has be be with the management with regard to administration, including the right of appointment, disciplinary powers, admission of students and the fees to be charged. At the school level, it is not possible to grant admissions on the basis of merit. It is no secret that the examination results at all levels of unaided private schools, notwithstanding the stringent regulations of the governmental authorities, are far superior to the results of the government-maintained schools. There is no compulsion on students tp attend private schools. The rush for admission is occasioned by the standards maintained in such schools, and recognition of the fact that State-run schools do not provide the same standards of education. The State says that it has no funds to establish institutions at the same level of excellence as private schools. But by curtailing the income of such private schools, it disables those schools from affording the best facilities because of a lack of funds. If this lowering of standards from excellence to a level of mediocrity is to be avoided, the State has to provide the difference which, therefore, brings us back in a vicious circle to the original problem viz. the lack of State funds. The solution would appear to lie in the States not using their scanty resources to prop up institutions that are able to otherwise maintain themselves out of the fees charged, but in improving the facilities and infrastructure of State-run schools and in subsidizing the fees payable by the students there. It is in the interest of the general public that more good quality schools are established; autonomy and non-regulation of the school administration in the right of appointment, admission of the students and the fee to be charged will ensure that more such institutions are established.

The private educational institutions have a personality of their own, and in order to maintain their atmosphere and traditions, it is but necessary that they must have the right to choose and select the students who can be admitted to their courses of studies.

Restriction under article 19(6)[28] can only be by way of a law and not by way of an office order without any authority of Law:

It is an equally well settled proposition of law that no citizen can be deprived of his fundamental right guaranteed under Article 19(1) of the Constitution in pursuance to an executive action without any authority of law. If any executive action operates to the prejudice of any person, it must be supported by legislative authority, i.e., a specific statutory provision or rule of law must authorise such an action. Executive instruction in the form of an administrative order unsupported by any statutory provision is not a justifiable restriction on fundamental rights.

*In **State of Madhya Pradesh and Anr. vs. Thakur Bharat Singh**[29], the Supreme Court has held, "All executive action which operates to the prejudice of any person must have the authority of law to support it, and the terms of Article 358[30] do not detract from the rule. Article 358 expressly authorises*

---

28 **Article 19 (1)(6) in The Constitution Of India 1949**
19. Protection of certain rights regarding freedom of speech etc
(1) All citizens shall have the right
(6) Nothing in sub clause (g) of the said clause shall affect the operation of any existing law in so far as it imposes, or prevent the State from making any law imposing, in the interests of the general public, reasonable restrictions on the exercise of the right conferred by the said sub clause, and, in particular, nothing in the said sub clause shall affect the operation of any existing law in so far as it relates to, or prevent the State from making any law relating to,
(i) the professional or technical qualifications necessary for practising any profession or carrying on any occupation, trade or business, or
(ii) the carrying on by the State, or by a corporation owned or controlled by the State, of any trade, business, industry or service, whether to the exclusion, complete or partial, of citizens or otherwise

29 (1967) 2 SCR 454

30 **Article 358 in The Constitution Of India 1949**
358. Suspension of provisions of Article 19 during emergencies
(1) While a Proclamation of Emergency declaring that the security of India or any part of the territory thereof is threatened by war or by external aggression is in operation, nothing in Article 19 shall restrict the power of the State as defined in Part III to make any law or to take any executive action which the State would but for the provisions contained in that Part be competent to make or to take, but any law so made shall, to the extent of the in competency, cease to have effect as soon as the Proclamation ceases to operate, except as respects things done or omitted to be done before the law so ceases to have effect: Provided that where such Proclamation of Emergency is in operation only in any part of the territory of India, any such law may be made, or any such executive action may be taken, under this article in relation to or in any State or Union territory in which or in any part of which the Proclamation of Emergency is not in operation, if and in so far as the security of India or any part of the territory thereof is threatened by activities in or in relation to the part of the territory of India in which the Proclamation

the State to take legislative or executive action provided such action was competent for the State to make or take. We have adopted under our Constitution not the continental system but the British system under which the rule of law prevails. Every Act done by the Government or by its officers must, if it is to operate to the prejudice of any person, be supported by some legislative authority."

In *Union of India Vs. Naveen Jindal and Anr.*[31] the Supreme Court has held as under:-

"The question, however, is as to whether the said executive instruction is "law" within the meaning of Article 13 of the Constitution of India. Article 13(3)(a) of the Constitution of India reads thus:

"13. (3)(a) 'law' includes any ordinance, order, bye-law, rule, regulation, notification, custom or usage having in the territory of India the force of law;"

A bare perusal of the said provision would clearly go to show that executive instructions would not fall within the aforementioned category. Such executive instructions may have the force of law for some other purposes; as for example those instructions which are issued as a supplement to the legislative power in terms of clause (1) of Article 77[32] of the Constitution of India. The necessity as regards determination of the said question has arisen as Parliament has not chosen to enact a statute which would confer at least a statutory right upon a citizen of India to fly the National Flag. An executive instruction issued by the appellant herein can any time be

---

of Emergency is in operation

(2) Nothing in clause (1) shall apply (a) to any law which does not contain a recital to the effect that such law is in relation to the Proclamation of Emergency in operation when it is made; or (b) to any executive action taken otherwise than under a law containing such a recital

31 (2004) 2 SCC 510

32 **Article 77 in The Constitution Of India 1949**
77. Conduct of business of the Government of India
(1) All executive action of the Government of India shall be expressed to be taken in the name of the President
(2) Orders and other instruments made and executed in the name of the President shall be authenticated in such manner as may be specified in rules to be made by the President, and the validity of an order or instrument which is so authenticated shall nor be called in question on the ground that it is not an order or instrument made or executed by the President
(3) The President shall make rules for the more convenient transaction of the business of the Government of India, and for the allocation among Ministers of the said business

replaced by another set of executive instructions and thus deprive Indian citizens from flying National Flag. Furthermore, such a question will also arise in the event if it be held that right to fly the National Flag is a fundamental or a natural right within the meaning of Article 19 of the Constitution of India; as for the purpose of regulating the exercise of right of freedom guaranteed under Articles 19(1)(a) to (e) and (g) a law must be made.

Right to impose conditions while granting recognition/affiliation cannot be used to destroy institutional autonomy:

Undoubtedly, the right to establish an educational institution is independent and separate from the right to recognition or affiliation and the statutory authorities can impose conditions for grant of affiliation or recognition; yet this power to impose a condition cannot completely destroy the institutional autonomy and the very object of establishment of the educational institution. In T.M.A. Pai Foundation (supra) the Supreme Court has held as under:-

"*Affiliation and recognition has to be available to every institution that fulfils the conditions for grant of such affiliation and recognition. The private institutions are right in submitting that it is not open to the Court to insist that statutory authorities should impose the terms of the scheme as a condition for grant of affiliation or recognition; this completely destroys the institutional autonomy and the very objective of establishment of the institution.*"

Children through their parents have a fundamental right to choose a school in which they wish to study under article 19(1)(a) of the Constitution:

Children below the age of six years through their parents have a fundamental right to education and health under Article 21 of constitution and the right to choose a particular or specialized school in which they wish to study under Article 19(1)(a) of the Constitution.

Parental school choice in its broadest sense means giving parents the ability to send their children to the school of their choice. The schools of choice often emphasize a particular subject or have a special philosophy of education. One school might emphasise Science or Art or Language or Sports. Another might offer a firm code of conduct or a rigorous traditional academic programme. Since colonial days, schools of choice have been part of the fabric of the city's education. The parents would certainly want their child's school to reflect the values of their family and community. For instance, Armed Forces personnel may like to get their wards admitted to Sainik or Air Force School. Similarly, Bengali or Gujarati parents may like to get their wards admitted in schools where primary education is imparted in their local language irrespective of the distance involved. In other words, they may want to choose a school that is a good fit for their child. After all, school choice can help give every child an excellent education and shape their future.

Decision by High Court:

Courts can quash[33] even a policy decision:

It is true that in policy matters, the Courts normally do not interfere. Yet it is settled law that if a policy is arbitrary or illegal or irrational or procedurally improper, then it is the bounden duty of the Court to quash it.

Private unaided recognized school managements have a fundamental right under Article 19(1)(g) of the Constitution to maximum autonomy in the day-to-day administration including the right to admit students. This right of private unaided schools has been recognized by an eleven judge Bench of the Supreme Court in T.M.A. Pai Foundation (supra). Subsequently, a Constitution Bench of the Supreme Court in P.A. Inamdar **and Ors.Vs. State of Maharashtra and Ors.**[34] has held that even non-minority unaided institutions have the unfettered fundamental right to devise the procedure to admit students subject to the said procedure being fair, reasonable and transparent. Even, in 2014, another Constitution Bench of the Supreme Court in Pramati Educational & Cultural Trust (Registered) & Ors.[35] reiterated that the content of the right under Article 19(1)(g) of the Constitution to establish and administer private educational institutions, as per the judgment of this Court in T.M.A. Pai Foundation, includes the right to admit students of their choice and autonomy of administration.

Undoubtedly, the right to administer is subject to reasonable restrictions under Article 19(6) of the Constitution. It is a settled proposition of law that the right to administer does not include the right to mal-administer.

Children below six years age have a fundamental right to education and health as also a right to choose a school under Article 19(1)(a) of the Constitution in which they wish to study. RTE Act, 2009 prescribes

---

33 **Meaning of Quash:**
  To annul or put an end to (a court order, indictment, or court proceedings).

34 AIR2005SC3226

35 (2014) 8 SCC 1

duty upon the State to ensure availability of neighbourhood schools. It nowhere stipulates that children would have to take admission only in a neighbourhood school or that children cannot take admissions in schools situated beyond their neighbourhood.

The power to choose a school has to primarily vest with the parents and not in the administration. In fact, the impugned office orders fail to consider the vitality as well as quality of the school and the specific needs of the individual families and students. School choice gives families freedom to choose any school that meets their needs regardless of its location. Court was of the opinion that by increasing parental choice and by granting schools the autonomy to admit students, the accountability of private schools can be ensured.

Consequently, in the opinion of the Court, children should have the option to go to a neighbourhood school, but their choice cannot be restricted to a school situated in their locality.

Court quashed the impugned office orders being violative of the fundamental right of the school management to maximum autonomy in day-to-day administration including the right to admit students as well as the fundamental right of children through their parents to choose a school, besides being contrary to Supreme Court and Division Bench judgments with **regard to seventy five per cent general nursery seats**.

Chapter-6

Right to Education[36]

Facts in Nutshell

Constitutional validity of the Right of Children to Free and Compulsory Education Act 2009 (35 of 2009) (in short, the Act) was challenged, which was enacted following the insertion of Article 21A[37] by the Constitution (Eighty-sixth Amendment) Act, 2002. Article 21A provides for free and compulsory education to all children of the age 6 to 14 years and also casts an obligation on the State to provide and ensure admission, attendance and completion of elementary education in such a manner that the State may by law determine. The Act is, therefore, enacted to provide for free and compulsory education to all children of the age 6 to 14 years and is anchored in the belief that the values of equality, social justice and democracy and the creation of just and humane society can be achieved only through a provision of inclusive elementary education to all the children. Provision of free and compulsory education of satisfactory quality to the children from disadvantaged groups and weaker sections, is not merely the responsibility of the schools run or supported by the appropriate government, but also of schools which are not dependent on government funds. Petitioners[38] wholeheartedly welcomed the introduction of Article 21A in the Constitution and acknowledged it as a revolutionary step providing universal elementary education for all the children. Controversy

---

36 Appellants: **Society for Un-aided Private Schools of Rajasthan Vs.** Respondent: **Union of India (UOI) and Anr.** AIR2012SC3445
Hon'ble Judges/Coram: S.H. Kapadia, C.J.I., Swatanter Kumar and K.S. Panicker Radhakrishnan, JJ.

37 **Article 21A of the Constitution**
Right to Education:
The State shall provide free and compulsory education to all children of the age of six to fourteen years in such manner as the State may, by law, determine

38 **Meaning of Petitioner:** A person who presents a Petition. (**Meaning of Petition:** A formal message requesting **something that is submitted to an authority**)

is not with regard to the validity of Article 21A, but mainly centers around its interpretation[39] and the validity of Sections 3[40], 12(1)(b)[41] and 12(1)(c) and some other related provisions of the Right to Education Act, 2009

---

39 **Meaning of Interpretation:**
   1. the act of interpreting; elucidation; explication.
   2. the meaning assigned to another's creative work, action, behavior, etc.

40 **Sections 3 of the Right to Education Act, 2009**
   3. Right of child to free and compulsory education.-
   1. Every child of the age of six to fourteen years shall have a right to free and compulsory education in a neighbourhood school till completion of elementary education.
   2. For the purpose of sub-section (1), no child shall be liable to pay any kind of fee or charges or expenses which may prevent him or her from pursuing and completing the elementary education:
   Provided that a child suffering from disability, as defined in clause (i) of section 2 of the Persons with Disabilities (Equal Opportunities, Protection and Full Participation) Act, 1996 (1 of 1996), shall have the right to pursue free and compulsory elementary education in accordance with the provisions of Chapter V of the said Act

41 **Sections 12 of the Right to Education Act, 2009**
   12. Extent of school's responsibility for free and compulsory education.-
   1. For the purposes of this Act, a school,--
      a. specified in sub-clause (i) of clause (n) of section 2 shall provide free and compulsory elementary education to all children admitted therein;
      b. specified in sub-clause (ii) of clause (n) of section 2 shall provide free and compulsory elementary education to such proportion of children admitted therein as its annual recurring aid or grants so received bears to its annual recurring expenses, subject to a minimum of twenty-five per cent.;
      c. specified in sub-clauses (iii) and (iv) of clause (n) of section 2 shall admit in class I, to the extent of at least twenty-five per cent. of the strength of that class, children belonging to weaker section and disadvantaged group in the neighbourhood and provide free and compulsory elementary education till its completion:
   Provided further that where a school specified in clause (n) of section 2 imparts pre-school education, the provisions of clauses (a) to (c) shall apply for admission to such pre-school education.
   2. The school specified in sub-clause (iv) of clause (n) of section 2 providing free and compulsory elementary education as specified in clause (c) of sub-section (1) shall be reimbursed expenditure so incurred by it to the extent of per-child-expenditure incurred by the State, or the actual amount charged from the child, whichever is less, in such manner as may be prescribed:
   Provided that such reimbursement shall not exceed per-child-expenditure incurred by a school specified in sub-clause (i) of clause (n) of section 2:
   Provided further that where such school is already under obligation to provide free education to a specified number of children on account of it having received any land, building, equipment or other facilities, either free of cost or at a concessional rate, such school shall not be entitled for reimbursement to the extent of such obligation.
   3. Every school shall provide such information as may be required by the appropriate Government or the local authority, as the case may be

which cast obligation on all elementary educational institutions to admit children of the age 6 to 14 years from their neighbourhood, on the principle of social inclusiveness.

Right to Education Act, 2009

Education is a process which engages many different actors: the one who provides education (the teacher, the owner of an educational institution, the parents), the one who receives education (the child, the pupil) and the one who is legally responsible for the one who receives education (the parents, the legal guardians, society and the State). These actors influence the right to education. The 2009 Act makes the Right of Children to Free and Compulsory Education justiciable[42]. **The 2009 Act envisages that each child must have access to a neighbourhood school.** The 2009 Act has been enacted keeping in mind the crucial role of Universal Elementary Education for strengthening the social fabric of democracy through provision of equal opportunities to all. The Directive Principles of State Policy[43] enumerated in our Constitution lay down that the State shall provide free and compulsory education to all children upto the age of 14 years. The said Act provides for right (entitlement) of children to free and compulsory admission, attendance and completion of elementary education in a neighbourhood school. The word "Free" in the long title[44] to the 2009 Act stands for removal by the State of any financial barrier that prevents a child from completing 8 years of schooling. The word "Compulsory" in that title stands for compulsion on the State and the parental duty to send children to school. To protect and give effect to this right of the child to

---

42 **Meaning of Justiciable:**
    1. Appropriate for or subject to court trial
    2. That can be settled by law or a court of law

43 The **Directive Principles of State Policy** are guidelines to the central and state governments of India, to be kept in mind while framing laws and policies. These provisions, contained in Part IV of the Constitution of India, are not enforceable by any court, but the principles laid down therein are considered fundamental in the governance of the country, making it the duty of the State to apply these principles in making laws to establish a just society in the country.

44 The **long title** (properly, the **title** in some jurisdictions) is the formal title appearing at the head of a statute (such as an Act of Parliament or of Congress) or other legislative instrument. The long title is intended to provide a summary description of the purpose or scope of the instrument; it contrasts with the short title, which is merely intended to provide a useful name when referring to it.

education as enshrined in Article 21[45] and Article 21A of the Constitution, the Parliament has enacted the 2009 Act.

The 2009 Act received the assent of the President on 26.8.2009. It came into force w.e.f. 1.4.2010. The provisions of this Act are intended not only to guarantee right to free and compulsory education to children, but it also envisages imparting of quality education by providing required infrastructure and compliance of specified norms and standards in the schools. The Preamble states that the 2009 Act stands enacted inter alia to provide for free and compulsory education to all children of the age of 6 to 14 years. The said Act has been enacted to give effect to Article 21A of the Constitution.

Scope of the Right to Education Act, 2009:

Section 3(1) of the 2009 Act provides that every child of the age of 6 to 14 years shall have a right to free and compulsory education in a neighbourhood school till completion of elementary education. Section 3(2) provides that no child shall be liable to pay any kind of fee or charges or expenses which may prevent him or her from pursuing and completing the elementary education. An educational institution is charitable. Advancement of education is a recognised head of charity. Section 3(2) has been enacted with the object of removing financial barrier which prevents a child from accessing education. The other purpose of enacting Section 3(2) is to prevent educational institutions charging capitation fees resulting in creation of a financial barrier which prevents a child from accessing or exercising its right to education which is now provided for vide Article 21A. Thus, Sub-section (2) provides that no child shall be liable to pay any kind of fee or charges or expenses which may prevent him or her from pursuing or completing the elementary education. Section 4 inter alia[46] provides for

---

45 **Article 21 in The Constitution Of India 1949**
   Protection of life and personal liberty: No person shall be deprived of his life or personal liberty except according to procedure established by law

46 **Section 4, Right of Children to Free and Compulsory Education Act, 2009**
   4. Special provisions for children not admitted to, or who have not completed, elementary education.-
   Where a child above six years of age has not been admitted in any school or though admitted, could not complete his or her elementary education, then, he or she shall be admitted in a class appropriate to his or her age:
   Provided that where a child is directly admitted in a class appropriate to his or her age, then, he or she shall, in order to be at par with others, have a right to receive special training, in such manner, and within such time-limits, as may be prescribed:

special provision for children not admitted to or who have not completed elementary education. Section 5[47] deals with the situation where there is no provision for completion of elementary education, then, in such an event, a child shall have a right to seek transfer to any other school, excluding the school specified in Sub-clauses (iii) and (iv) of Clause (n) of Section 2, for completing his or her elementary education. Section 6[48] imposes an obligation on the appropriate government and local authority to establish a school within such areas or limits of neighbourhood, as may be prescribed, where it is not so established, within 3 years from the commencement of the 2009 Act. The emphasis is on providing "neighbourhood school" facility to the children at the Gram Panchayat level. Chapter Section 12(1)

Provided further that a child so admitted to elementary education shall be entitlted to free education till completion of elementary education even after fourteen years

47　**Section 5, Right of Children to Free and Compulsory Education Act, 2009**
　　5. Right of transfer to other school.-
　　1. Where in a school, there is no provision for completion of elementary education, a child shall have a right to seek transfer to any other school, excluding the school specified in sub-clauses (iii) and (iv) of clause (n) of section 2, for completing his or her elementary education.
　　2. Where a child is required to move from one school to another, either within a State or outside, for any reason whatsoever, such child shall have a right to seek transfer to any other school, excluding the school specified in sub-clauses (iii) and (iv) of clause (n) of section 2, for completing his or her elementary education.
　　3. For seeking admission in such other school, the Head-teacher or in-charge of the school where such child was last admitted, shall immediately issue the transfer certificate:
　　Provided that delay in producing transfer certificate shall not be a ground for either delaying or denying admission in such other school:
　　Provided further that the Head-teacher or in-charge of the school delaying issuance of transfer certificate shall be liable for disciplinary action under the service rules applicable to him or her

48　**Section 6, Right of Children to Free and Compulsory Education Act, 2009**
　　6. Duty of appropriate Government and local authority to establish school-
　　For carrying out the provisions of this Act, the appropriate Government and the local authority shall establish, within such area or limits of neighbourhood, as may be prescribed, a school, where it is not so established, within a period of three years from the commencement of this Act

(c)[49] read with Section 2(n)(iii)[50] and (iv) mandates that every recognised school imparting elementary education, even if it is an unaided school, not receiving any kind of aid or grant to meet its expenses from the appropriate government or the local authority, is obliged to admit in Class I, to the extent of at least 25% of the strength of that class, children belonging to weaker section and disadvantaged group in the neighbourhood and provide free and compulsory elementary education till its completion. As

---

49   **Section 12, Right of Children to Free and Compulsory Education Act, 2009**
  12. Extent of school's responsibility for free and compulsory education.-
  1. For the purposes of this Act, a school,--
      a. specified in sub-clause (i) of clause (n) of section 2 shall provide free and compulsory elementary education to all children admitted therein;
      b. specified in sub-clause (ii) of clause (n) of section 2 shall provide free and compulsory elementary education to such proportion of children admitted therein as its annual recurring aid or grants so received bears to its annual recurring expenses, subject to a minimum of twenty-five per cent.;
      c. specified in sub-clauses (iii) and (iv) of clause (n) of section 2 shall admit in class I, to the extent of at least twenty-five per cent. of the strength of that class, children belonging to weaker section and disadvantaged group in the neighbourhood and provide free and compulsory elementary education till its completion:
  Provided further that where a school specified in clause (n) of section 2 imparts pre-school education, the provisions of clauses (a) to (c) shall apply for admission to such pre-school education.
  2. The school specified in sub-clause (iv) of clause (n) of section 2 providing free and compulsory elementary education as specified in clause (c) of sub-section (1) shall be reimbursed expenditure so incurred by it to the extent of per-child-expenditure incurred by the State, or the actual amount charged from the child, whichever is less, in such manner as may be prescribed:
  Provided that such reimbursement shall not exceed per-child-expenditure incurred by a school specified in sub-clause (i) of clause (n) of section 2:
  Provided further that where such school is already under obligation to provide free education to a specified number of children on account of it having received any land, building, equipment or other facilities, either free of cost or at a concessional rate, such school shall not be entitled for reimbursement to the extent of such obligation.
  3. Every school shall provide such information as may be required by the appropriate Government or the local authority, as the case may be

50   **Section 2 (n), Right of Children to Free and Compulsory Education Act, 2009**
  n.   "school" means any recognised school imparting elementary education and includes--
          i. a school established, owned or controlled by the appropriate Government or a local authority;
          ii. an aided school receiving aid or grants to meet whole or part of its expenses from the appropriate Government or the local authority;
          iii. a school belonging to specified category; and
          iv. an unaided school not receiving any kind of aid or grants to meet its expenses from the appropriate Government or the local authority

per the proviso, if the School is imparting pre-school education, the same regime would apply. By virtue of Section12(2) the unaided school which has not received any land, building, equipment or other facilities, either free of cost or at concessional rate, would be entitled for reimbursement of the expenditure incurred by it to the extent of per child expenditure incurred by the State, or the actual amount charged from the child, whichever is less, in such manner as may be prescribed. Such reimbursement shall not exceed per child expenditure incurred by a school established, owned or controlled by the appropriate government or a local authority. Section 13[51] envisages that no school or person shall, while admitting a child, collect any capitation fee and subject the child or his or her parents to any screening procedure. Section 15[52] mandates that a child shall be admitted in a school at the commencement of the academic year or within the prescribed extended period. Sections 16[53] and 17[54] provide for prohibition of holding back and expulsion and of physical punishment or mental harassment to

---

51 **Section 13, Right of Children to Free and Compulsory Education Act, 2009**
   13. No capitation fee and screening procedure for admission.-
   1. No school or person shall, while admitting a child, collect any capitation fee and subject the child or his or her parents or guardian to any screening procedure.
   2. Any school or person, if in contravention of the provisions of sub-section (1),--
      a. receives capitation fee, shall be punishable with fine which may extend to ten times the capitation fee charged;
      b. subjects a child to screening procedure, shall be punishable with fine which may extend to twenty-five thousand rupees for the first contravention and fifty thousand rupees for each subsequent contraventions

52 **Section 15, Right of Children to Free and Compulsory Education Act, 2009**
   15. No denial of admission.-
   A child shall be admitted in a school at the commencement of the academic year or within such extended period as may be prescribed:
   Provided that no child shall be denied admission if such admission is sought subsequent to the extended period:
   Provided further that any child admitted after the extended period shall complete his studies in such manner as may be prescribed by the appropriate Government

53 **Section 16, Right of Children to Free and Compulsory Education Act, 2009**
   16. Prohibition of holding back and expulsion.-
   No child admitted in a school shall be held back in any class or expelled from school till the completion of elementary education

54 **Section 17, Right of Children to Free and Compulsory Education Act, 2009**
   17. Prohibition of physical punishment and mental harassment to child.-
   1. No child shall be subjected to physical punishment or mental harassment.
   2. Whoever contravenes the provisions of sub-section (1) shall be liable to disciplinary action under the service rules applicable to such person

a child. Section 18[55] postulates[56] that after the commencement of the 2009 Act no school, other than the excepted category, can be established or can function without obtaining a certificate of recognition from the appropriate authority. The appropriate authority shall be obliged to issue the certificate of recognition within the prescribed period specifying the conditions there for, if the school fulfills the norms and standards specified under

---

55 **Section 18, Right of Children to Free and Compulsory Education Act, 2009**
   18. No School to be established without obtaining certificate of recognition.-
   1. No school, other than a school established, owned or controlled by the appropriate Government or the local authority, shall, after the commencement of this Act, be established or function, without obtaining a certificate of recognition from such authority, by making an application in such form and manner, as may be prescribed.
   2. The authority prescribed under sub-section (1) shall issue the certificate of recognition in such form, within such period, in such manner, and subject to such conditions, as may be prescribed:
   Provided that no such recognition shall be granted to a school unless it fulfils norms and standards specified under section 19
   3. On the contravention of the conditions of recognition, the prescribed authority shall, by an order in writing, withdraw recognition:
   Provided that such order shall contain a direction as to which of the neighbourhood school, the children studying in the derecognised school, shall be admitted:
   Provided further that no recognition shall be so withdrawn without giving an opportunity of being heard to such school, in such manner, as may be prescribed.
   4. With effect from the date of withdrawal of the recognition under sub-section (3), no such school shall continue to function.
   5. Any person who establishes or runs a school without obtaining certificate of recognition, or continues to run a school after withdrawal of recognition, shall be liable to fine which may extend to one lakh rupees and in case of continuing contraventions, to a fine of ten thousand rupees for each day during which such contravention continues

56 **Meaning of Postulate:**
   1. To make claim for; demand.
   2. To assume or assert the truth, reality, or necessity of, especially as a basis of an argument

Sections 19[57] and 25[58] read with the Schedule to the 2009 Act. In the event of contravention of the conditions of recognition, the prescribed authority can withdraw recognition after giving an opportunity of being heard to such school. The order of withdrawal of recognition should provide a direction to transfer the children studying in the de-recognised school to be admitted to the specified neighbourhood school. Upon withdrawal of recognition, the de-recognised school cannot continue to function, failing which, is liable to pay fine as per Section 19(5). If any person establishes or runs a school without obtaining certificate of recognition, or continues to run a school after withdrawal of the recognition, shall be liable to pay fine as specified in Section 19(5). Section 22[59] postulates that the School

---

57 **Section 19, Right of Children to Free and Compulsory Education Act, 2009**
19. Norms and standards for school.-
   1. No school shall be established,, or recognised, under section 18, unless it fulfils the norms and standards specified in the Schedule.
   2. Where a school established before the commencement of this Act does not fulfill the norms and standards specified in the Schedule, it shall take steps to fulfill such norms and standards at its own expenses, within a period of three years from the date of such commencement.
   3. Where a school fails to fulfil the norms and standards within the period specified under sub-section (2), the authority prescribed under sub-section (1) of section 18 shall withdraw recognition granted to such school in the manner specified under sub-section (3) thereof.
   4. With effect from the date of withdrawal of recognition under sub-section (3), no school shall continue to function.
   5. Any person who continues to run a school after the recognition is withdrawn, shall be liable to fine which may extend to one lakh rupees and in case of continuing contraventions, to a fine of ten thousand rupees for each day during which such contravention continues

58 **Section 25, Right of Children to Free and Compulsory Education Act, 2009**
25. Pupil-Teacher Ratio.-
   1. Within six months from the date of commencement of this Act, the appropriate Government and the local authority shall ensure that the Pupil-Teacher Ratio, as specified in the Schedule, is maintained in each school.
   2. For the purpose of maintaining the Pupil-Teacher Ratio under sub-section (1), no teacher posted in a school shall be made to serve in any other school or office or deployed for any non-educational purpose, other than those specified in section 27

59 **Section 22, Right of Children to Free and Compulsory Education Act, 2009**
22. School Development Plan.-
   1. Every School Management Committee, constituted under sub-section (1) of section 21, shall prepare a School Development Plan, in such manner as may be prescribed.
   2. The School Development Plan so prepared under sub-section (1) shall be the basis for the plans and grants to be made by the appropriate Government or local authority, as the case may be

Management Committee constituted under Section 21[60], shall prepare a School Development Plan in the prescribed manner. Section 22(2) provides that the School Development Plan so prepared shall be the basis for the grants to be made by the appropriate government or local authority, as the case may be. That plan, however, cannot have any impact on consideration of application for grant of recognition for establishing an unaided school. To ensure that teachers should contribute in imparting quality education in the school itself, Section 28[61] imposes total prohibition on them to engage in private tuition or private teaching activities. Section 32[62] thus provides that any person having grievance relating to the right of child under the

---

60 **Section 21, Right of Children to Free and Compulsory Education Act, 2009**
    21. School Management Committee.-
    1. A school, other than a school specified in sub-clause (iv) of clause (n) of section 2, shall constitute a School Management Committee consisting of the elected representatives of the local authority, parents or guardians of children admitted in such school and teachers:
    Provided that at least three-fourth of members of such Committee shall be parents or guardians:
    Provided further that proportionate representation shall be given to the parents or guardians of children belonging to disadvantaged group and weaker section:
    Provided also that fifty per cent. of Members of such Committee shall be women.
    2. The School Management Committee shall perform the following functions, namely:--
        a. monitor the working of the school;
        b. prepare and recommend school development plan;
        c. monitor the utilisation of the grants received from the appropriate Government or local authority or any other source; and
        d. perform such other functions as may be prescribed

61 **Section 28, Right of Children to Free and Compulsory Education Act, 2009**
    28. Prohibition of private tuition by teacher.-
    No teacher shall engage himself or herself in private tuition or private teaching activity

62 **Section 32, Right of Children to Free and Compulsory Education Act, 2009**
    32. Redressal of grievances.-
    1. Notwithstanding anything contained in section 31, any person having any grievance relating to the right of a child under this Act may make a written complaint to the local authority having jurisdiction.
    2. After receiving the complaint under sub-section (1), the local authority shall decide the matter within a period of three months after affording a reasonable opportunity of being heard to the parties concerned.
    3. Any person aggrieved by the decision of the local authority may prefer an appeal to the State Commission for Protection of Child Rights or the authority prescribed under sub-section (3) of section 31, as the case may be.
    4. The appeal preferred under sub-section (3) shall be decided by State Commission for Protection of Child Rights or the authority prescribed under sub-section (3) of section 31, as the case may be, as provided under clause (c) of sub-section (1) of section 31

2009 Act, may make a written complaint to the local authority having jurisdiction, who in turn is expected to decide it within three months after affording a reasonable opportunity of being heard to the parties concerned. In addition, in terms of Section 31[63], the Commissions constituted under the provisions of the Commissions for Protection of Child Rights Act, 2005 can monitor the child's right to education, so as to safeguard the right of the child upon receiving any complaint in that behalf relating to free and compulsory education.

By virtue of the 2009 Act, all schools established prior to the commencement of the said Act are thus obliged to fulfill the norms and standards specified in Sections 25, 26[64] and the Schedule of that Act. The State is also expected to first weed out those schools which are non-performing, or under-performing or non-compliance schools and upon closure of such schools, the students and the teaching and non-teaching staff thereof should be transferred to the neighbourhood school.

Right to education is a fundamental right:

63   **Section 31, Right of Children to Free and Compulsory Education Act, 2009**
   31. Monitoring of child's right to education.-
   1. The National Commission for Protection of Child Rights constituted under section 3, or, as the case may be, the State Commission for Protection of Child Rights constituted under section 17, of the Commissions for Protection of Child Rights Act, 2005 (4 of 2006), shall, in addition to the functions assigned to them under that Act, also perform the following functions, namely:--
      a. examine and review the safeguards for rights provided by or under this Act and recommend measures for their effective implementation;
      b. inquire into complaints relating to child's right to free and compulsory education; and
      c. take necessary steps as provided under sections 15 and 24 of the said Commissions for Protection of Child Rights Act.
   2. The said Commissions shall, while inquiring into any matters relating to child's right to free and compulsory education under clause (c) of sub-section (1), have the same powers as assigned to them respectively under sections 14 and 24 of the said Commissions for Protection of Child Rights Act.
   3. Where the State Commission for Protection of Child Rights has not been constituted in a State, the appropriate Government may, for the purpose of performing the functions specified in clauses (a) to (c) of sub-section (1), constitute such authority, in such manner and subject to such terms and conditions, as may be prescribed

64   **Section 26, Right of Children to Free and Compulsory Education Act, 2009**
   26. Filling up vacancies of teachers.-
   The appointing authority, in relation to a school established, owned, controlled or substantially financed by funds provided directly or indirectly by the appropriate Government or by a local authority, shall ensure that vacancy of teacher in a school under its control shall not exceed ten per cent/of the total sanctioned strength

In *Mohini Jain v. State of Karnataka and Ors.*[65], Supreme Court held that the right to education is a fundamental right guaranteed under Article 21 of the Constitution and that dignity of individuals cannot be assured unless accompanied by right to education and that charging of **capitation fee**[66] for admission to educational institutions would amount to denial of citizens' right to education and is violative of Article 14[67] of the Constitution. The ratio laid down in Mohini Jain was questioned in *Unni Krishnan, J.P. and Ors. v. State of A.P. and Ors.*[68] contending that if the judgment in Mohini Jain was given effect to, many of the private educational institutions would have to be closed down. Mohini Jain was affirmed[69] in Unni Krishnan to the extent of holding that the right to education flows from Article 21 of the Constitution and charging of capitation fee was illegal. The Court partly overruled[70] Mohini Jain and held that the right to free education is available only to children until they complete the age of 14 years and after that obligation of the State to provide education would be subject to the limits of its economic capacity and development. Private unaided recognized/affiliated educational institutions running professional courses were held entitled to charge the fee higher than that charged by government institutions for similar courses but that such a fee should not exceed the maximum limit fixed by the State. The Court also formulated a scheme and directed every authority to impose that scheme upon institutions seeking recognition/affiliation, even if they are unaided institutions. Unni Krishnan introduced the concept of *"free seats"* and *"payment seats"* and ordered that private unaided educational institutions should not add any further conditions and were held bound by the scheme. *Unni Krishnan also recognized the right to education as a fundamental right guaranteed under Article21 of the Constitution and held that the right is available to children until they complete the age of 14 years.*

---

65   (1992) 3 SCC 666

66   In the context of Indian law, a capitation fee refers to the collection of payment by educational bodies not advertised in the prospectus of the institution, usually in exchange for admission to the institution

67   **Article 14 in The Constitution Of India 1949**
14. Equality before law: The State shall not deny to any person equality before the law or the equal protection of the laws within the territory of India Prohibition of discrimination on grounds of religion, race, caste, sex or place of birth

68   (1993) 1 SCC 645

69   **Meaning of Affirm:** To declare solemnly and formally but not under oath.

70   **Meaning of Overrule:** To declare null and void; reverse

In *T.M.A. Pai Foundation and Ors. v. State of Karnataka and Ors.*[71] examined the correctness of the ratio laid down in Unni Krishnan and also the validity of the scheme. Pai Foundation acknowledged the right of all citizens to practice any profession, trade or business under Article 19(1) (g)[72] and Article 26[73] and held those rights would be subject to the provisions

---

71 (2002) 8 SCC 481

72 **Article 19 in The Constitution Of India 1949**
19. Protection of certain rights regarding freedom of speech etc
(1) All citizens shall have the right
(a) to freedom of speech and expression;
(b) to assemble peaceably and without arms;
(c) to form associations or unions;
(d) to move freely throughout the territory of India;
(e) to reside and settle in any part of the territory of India; and
(f) omitted
(g) to practise any profession, or to carry on any occupation, trade or business
(2) Nothing in sub clause (a) of clause (1) shall affect the operation of any existing law, or prevent the State from making any law, in so far as such law imposes reasonable restrictions on the exercise of the right conferred by the said sub clause in the interests of the sovereignty and integrity of India, the security of the State, friendly relations with foreign States, public order, decency or morality or in relation to contempt of court, defamation or incitement to an offence
(3) Nothing in sub clause (b) of the said clause shall affect the operation of any existing law in so far as it imposes, or prevent the State from making any law imposing, in the interests of the sovereignty and integrity of India or public order, reasonable restrictions on the exercise of the right conferred by the said sub clause
(4) Nothing in sub clause (c) of the said clause shall affect the operation of any existing law in so far as it imposes, or prevent the State from making any law imposing, in the interests of the sovereignty and integrity of India or public order or morality, reasonable restrictions on the exercise of the right conferred by the said sub clause
(5) Nothing in sub clauses (d) and (e) of the said clause shall affect the operation of any existing law in so far as it imposes, or prevent the State from making any law imposing, reasonable restrictions on the exercise of any of the rights conferred by the said sub clauses either in the interests of the general public or for the protection of the interests of any Scheduled Tribe
(6) Nothing in sub clause (g) of the said clause shall affect the operation of any existing law in so far as it imposes, or prevent the State from making any law imposing, in the interests of the general public, reasonable restrictions on the exercise of the right conferred by the said sub clause, and, in particular, nothing in the said sub clause shall affect the operation of any existing law in so far as it relates to, or prevent the State from making any law relating to,
(i) the professional or technical qualifications necessary for practising any profession or carrying on any occupation, trade or business, or
(ii) the carrying on by the State, or by a corporation owned or controlled by the State, of any trade, business, industry or service, whether to the exclusion, complete or partial, of citizens or otherwise

73 **Article 26 in The Constitution Of India 1949**

that were placed under Article 19(6) and 26(a) and the rights of minority to establish and administer educational institutions under Article 30[74] was also upheld. Unni Krishnan scheme was held unconstitutional, but it was ordered that there should be no capitation fee or profiteering and reasonable surplus to meet the cost of expansion and augmentation of facilities would not mean profiteering. Further, it was also ordered that the expression "education" in all the Articles of the Constitution would mean and include education at all levels, from primary education level up to post graduate level and the expression "educational institutions" would mean institutions that impart education as understood in the Constitution.

Question before the Supreme Court:

The State may decide to provide free and compulsory education to all children of the specified age through its own schools or through government aided schools or through unaided private schools. The question was whether such a law transgresses[75] any constitutional limitation?

Article 21A of the Constitution of India:

Article 21A: It provides that the State shall provide free and compulsory education to all children of the age of 6 to 14 years in such manner as the State may, by law, determine. Thus, under the said Article, the obligation is on the State to provide free and compulsory education to all children of specified age. However, under the said Article, the manner in which the

---

26. **Freedom to manage religious affairs:** Subject to public order, morality and health, every religious denomination or any section thereof shall have the right
    (a) to establish and maintain institutions for religious and charitable purposes;
    (b) to manage its own affairs in matters of religion;
    (c) to own and acquire movable and immovable property; and
    (d) to administer such property in accordance with law

74 **Article 30 in The Constitution Of India 1949**
    30. Right of minorities to establish and administer educational institutions
    (1) All minorities, whether based on religion or language, shall have the right to establish and administer educational institutions of their choice
    (1A) In making any law providing for the compulsory acquisition of any property of an educational institution established and administered by a minority, referred to in clause (1), the State shall ensure that the amount fixed by or determined under such law for the acquisition of such property is such as would not restrict or abrogate the right guaranteed under that clause
    (2) The state shall not, in granting aid to educational institutions, discriminate against any educational institution on the ground that it is under the management of a minority, whether based on religion or language

75 **Meaning of Transgress:** To go beyond or over (a limit or boundary); exceed or overstep

said obligation will be discharged by the State has been left to the State to determine by law.

Under Article 21A of the Constitution, right is given to the State to provide by law "free and compulsory education". Thus, Article 21A contemplates[76] right to education flowing from the law to be made which is the 2009 Act, which is child centric and not institution centric. Thus, as stated, Article 21A provides that the State shall provide free and compulsory education to all children of the specified age in such manner as the State may, by law, determine. The manner in which this obligation will be discharged by the State has been left to the State to determine by law. The 2009 Act is thus enacted in terms of Article21A. It has been enacted primarily to remove all barriers (including financial barriers) which impede access to education.

A child who is denied right to access education is not only deprived of his right to live with dignity (Article 21 of the Constitution), he is also deprived of his right to freedom of speech and expression enshrined in Article 19(1)(a). The 2009 Act seeks to remove all those barriers including financial and psychological barriers which a child belonging to the weaker section and disadvantaged group has to face while seeking admission.

To put an obligation on the unaided non-minority school to admit 25% children in class I under Section 12(1)(c) cannot be termed as an unreasonable restriction. Such a law cannot be said to transgress any constitutional limitation. The object of the 2009 Act is to remove the barriers faced by a child who seeks admission to class I and not to restrict the freedom under Article 19(1)(g).

Decision by Supreme Court:

Is the Right to Education Act, 2009 intended to apply to unaided minority schools? The intention of the Parliament is that the minority educational institution referred to in Article 30(1) is a separate category of institutions which needs protection of Article 30(1) and viewed in that light court was of the view that unaided minority schools needs special protection under Article 30(1). Article 30(1) is not conditional as Article 19(1)(g). In a sense, it is absolute as the Constitution framers thought that it was the duty of the Government of the day to protect the minorities in the matter of preservation of culture, language and script via establishment of educational institutions for religious and charitable purposes (See: Article 26). Reservations of 25% in such unaided minority schools result

---

76 **Meaning of Contemplate:** To look at attentively and thoughtfully

in changing the character of the schools if right to establish and administer such schools flows from the right to conserve the language, script or culture, which right is conferred on such unaided minority schools. Thus, the 2009 Act including Section 12(1)(c) violates the right conferred on such unaided minority schools under Article 30(1). The 2009 Act is enacted to remove barriers such as financial barriers which restrict his/her access to education. It is enacted pursuant to Article 21A. Court held that the 2009 Act is constitutionally valid qua **aided minority schools**.

Court further held that the Right of Children to Free and Compulsory Education Act, 2009 is constitutionally valid and shall apply to the following:

(i) a school established, owned or controlled by the appropriate Government or a local authority;

(ii) an aided school including aided minority school(s) receiving aid or grants to meet whole or part of its expenses from the appropriate Government or the local authority;

(iii) a school belonging to specified category; and

(iv) an unaided non-minority school not receiving any kind of aid or grants to meet its expenses from the appropriate Government or the local authority.

Chapter-7

Equality of status and of opportunity[77]

Facts in Nutshell

In every free country which has adopted a system of governance through democratic principles, the people have their fundamental inalienable[78] rights and enjoy the recognition of inherent dignity and of equality analogous to the rights proclaimed in the 'Bill of Rights' in U.S.A., the 'Rights of Man' in the French Constitution of 1971 and 'Declaration of Human Rights' etc. Our Constitution is unquestionably unique in its character and assimilation having its notable aspirations contained in 'Fundamental Rights'[79] (in part III) through which the illumination of Constitutional rights comes to us not through an artless window glass but refracted with the enhanced intensity and beauty by prismatic interpretation of the Constitutional provisions dealing with equal distribution of justice in the social, political and economic spheres. Though forty-five years from the commencement of the Indian independence after the end of British paramount and forty-two years from the advent of our Constitution have marched on, the tormenting enigma that often nags the people of India is whether the principle of **'equality of status and of opportunity'** to be equally provided to all the citizens of our country from cradle to grave

---

77 Appellants: **Indra Sawhney Vs.** Respondent: **Union of India (UOI) and Ors.**
1992Supp(3)SCC217
Hon'ble Judges/Coram: Harilal Jekisundas Kania, M. N. Venkatachaliah, S. Ratnavel Pandian, Dr. T. K. Thommen, A. M. Ahmadii, Kuldip Singh, P. B. Sawant, R. M. Sahai and B.P. Jeevan Reddy, JJ.

78 **Meaning of Inalienable:** That cannot be transferred to another or others

79 **Meaning of Fundamental Rights:** The Fundamental Rights are defined as basic human freedoms which every Indian citizen has the right to enjoy for a proper and harmonious development of personality. These rights universally apply to all citizens, irrespective of race, place of birth, religion, caste, creed, colour or gender. Aliens (persons who are not citizens) are also considered in matters like equality before law. They are enforceable by the courts, subject to certain restrictions

is satisfactorily consummated[80] and whether the clarion[81] of *equality of opportunity in matters of public employment'* enshrined in *Article 16(4)*[82] *of the Constitution of India has been called into action?*

The founding fathers of our Constitution have designedly couched Articles 14[83], 15[84] and 16 in comprehensive phraseology so that the frail

---

80   **Meaning of Consummated:** To complete (a marriage) legally by sexual intercourse

81   **Meaning of Clarion:**
  1.   Clear and ringing; inspiring
  2.   To proclaim loudly

82   **Article 16 in The Constitution Of India 1949**
  16. Equality of opportunity in matters of public employment
  (1) There shall be equality of opportunity for all citizens in matters relating to employment or appointment to any office under the State
  (2) No citizen shall, on grounds only of religion, race, caste, sex, descent, place of birth, residence or any of them, be ineligible for, or discriminated against in respect or, any employment or office under the State
  (3) Nothing in this article shall prevent Parliament from making any law prescribing, in regard to a class or classes of employment or appointment to an office under the Government of, or any local or other authority within, a State or Union territory, any requirement as to residence within that State or Union territory prior to such employment or appointment
  (4) Nothing in this article shall prevent the State from making any provision for the reservation of appointments or posts in favor of any backward class of citizens which, in the opinion of the State, is not adequately represented in the services under the State
  (5) Nothing in this article shall affect the operation of any law which provides that the incumbent of an office in connection with the affairs of any religious or denominational institution or any member of the governing body thereof shall be a person professing a particular religion or belonging to a particular denomination

83   **Article 14 in The Constitution Of India 1949**
  14. Equality before law: The State shall not deny to any person equality before the law or the equal protection of the laws within the territory of India Prohibition of discrimination on grounds of religion, race, caste, sex or place of birth

84   **Article 15 in The Constitution Of India 1949**
  15. Prohibition of discrimination on grounds of religion, race, caste, sex or place of birth
  (1) The State shall not discriminate against any citizen on grounds only of religion, race, caste, sex, place of birth or any of them
  (2) No citizen shall, on grounds only of religion, race, caste, sex, place of birth or any of them, be subject to any disability, liability, restriction or condition with regard to
  (a) access to shops, public restaurants, hotels and palaces of public entertainment; or
  (b) the use of wells, tanks, bathing ghats, roads and places of public resort maintained wholly or partly out of State funds or dedicated to the use of the general public
  (3) Nothing in this article shall prevent the State from making any special provision for women and children
  (4) Nothing in this article or in clause (2) of Article 29 shall prevent the State from

and emaciated section of the people living in poverty, rearing in obscurity, possessing no wealth or influence, having no education, much less higher education and suffering from social repression and oppression should not be denied of equality before the law and equal protection of the laws and equal opportunity in the matters of public employment or subjected to any prohibition of discrimination on grounds of religion, race, caste, sex or place of birth. To achieve the objectives, the Government have enacted innumerable social welfare legislations and geared up social reformative measures for uplifting the social and economic development of the disadvantaged section of people. True, a rapid societal transformation and profusion of other progressive changes are taking place, yet a major section of the people living below the poverty line and suffering from social ostracism still stand far behind and lack in every respect to keep pace with the advanced section of the people. The undignified social status and sub human living conditions leave an indelible impression that their forlorn hopes for equality in every sphere of life are only a myth rather than a reality. It is verily believed - rightly too - that the one and only peerless[85] way and indeed a most important and promising way to achieve the equal status and equal opportunity is only by means of constitutional justice so that all the citizens of this country irrespective of their religion, race, caste, sex, place of birth or any of them may achieve the goal of an egalitarian[86] society.

The Concept of Reservation

The Constitution permits the State to adopt such affirmative[87] action as it deems necessary to uplift the backward classes of citizens to levels of equality with the rest of our countrymen. The backward classes of citizens have been in the past denied access to Government services on account of their inability to compete effectively in open selections on the basis of merits. It is, therefore, open to the Government to reserve a certain number of seats in places of learning and public services in favour of the Scheduled Castes and the Scheduled Tribes and other backward classes to

---

making any special provision for the advancement of any socially and educationally backward classes of citizens or for the Scheduled Castes and the Scheduled Tribes

85 **Meaning of Peerless:** Being such as to have no match; incomparable.

86 **Meaning of Egalitarian:** Affirming, promoting, or characterized by belief in equal political, economic, social, and civil rights for all people

87 **Meaning of Affirmative:**
   1. Asserting that something is true or correct, as with the answer "yes"
   2. Giving assent or approval; confirming

the exclusion of all others, irrespective of merits.

Reservation is not an end in itself. It is a means to achieve equality. The policy of reservation adopted to achieve that end must, therefore, be consistent with the objective in view. Reservation must not outlast its constitutional object, and must not allow a vested interest to develop and perpetuate itself. There will be no need for reservation or preferential treatment once equality is achieved. Achievement and preservation of equality for all classes of people, irrespective of their birth, creed, faith or language is one of the noble ends to which the Constitution is dedicated. Every reservation founded on benign discrimination, and justifiably adopted to achieve the constitutional mandate of equality, must necessarily be a transient passage to that end. It is temporary in concept, limited in duration, conditional in application and specific in object. Reservation must contain within itself the seeds of its termination. Any attempt to perpetuate reservation and upset the constitutional mandate of equality is destructive of liberty and fraternity[88] and all the basic values enshrined[89] in the Constitution. A balance has to be maintained between the competing values and the rival claims and interests so as to achieve equality and freedom for all.

To what extent can the reservation be made?

It was for the first time that Supreme Court in Balaji case[90] has indicated broadly that the reservation should be less than 50% and the question how much less than 50% would depend on the relevant prevailing circumstances in each case. Though in Balaji, the issue in dispute related only to the reservation prescribed for admissions in the medical college from the educationally and socially backward classes, scheduled castes and scheduled tribes as being violative of Article 15(4), Supreme Court after expressing its view that it should be less than 50% observed further that "the provisions of Article 15(4) are similar to those of Article 16(4). Therefore, what is true in regard to Article 15(4) is equally true in regard to Article 16(4). Reservation made under Article 16(4) beyond the permissible and legitimate limits would be liable to be challenged as a fraud on the Constitution. To say in other words, Balaji case has fixed that the

---

88 **Meaning of Fraternity:**
    1. A body of people associated for a common purpose or interest, such as a guild.
    2. A group of people joined by similar backgrounds, occupations, interests, or tastes

89 **Meaning of Enshrined:**
    1. To enclose in or as if in a shrine.
    2. To cherish as sacred

90 M.R. Balaji v. State of Mysore 1963 (Suppl.) 1 SCR 439

maximum limit of reservation all put together should not exceed 50% and if it exceeds, it is nothing but a fraud on the Constitution. In fact, Article 16(4) itself does not limit the power of the Government in making the reservation to any maximum percentage; but it depends upon the quantum of adequate representation required in the Services.

Issues involved in the Case:

The equal opportunity in the matters of public employment. The constitutional provision, namely, Clause (4) of Article 16 proclaiming a "Fundamental Right" enacted about 42 years ago for providing equality of opportunity in matters of public employment to people belonging to any backward class has still not been given effect to in services under the Union of India and many more States. A number of Backward Classes Commissions have been appointed in some of the States, the recommendations of which have been repeatedly subjected to judicial scrutiny. Though the President of India appointed the second Backward Classes Commission under the chairmanship of Shri B.P. Mandal as far back as 1st January, 1979 and the Report was submitted in December, 1980, no effective steps were taken for its implementation till the issuance of the two office Memorandum[91]. Having regard to this appalling situation and the pathetic condition of the backward classes, for the first time the Union of India has issued the Office Memorandum (hereinafter called the 'O.M.') in August 1991 and thereafter an amended O.M. in September 1991 on the basis of the recommendations of the Mandal Commission[92].

Immediately after the announcement of the acceptance of the Report of the Mandal Commission, there were unabated pro as well as anti reservation agitations[93] and violent societal disturbances virtually paralysing the normal life. It was unfortunate and painful to note that some youths who

---

91 **Meaning of Memorandum:** A short written statement outlining the terms of an agreement, transaction, or contract

92 The **Mandal Commission** was established in India in 1979 by the Janata Party government under Prime Minister Morarji Desai with a mandate to "identify the socially or educationally backward." It was headed by Indian parliamentarian B.P. Mandal to consider the question of seat reservations and quotas for people to redress caste discrimination, and used eleven social, economic, and educational indicators to determine backwardness

93 **Meaning of Agitation:**
1. The act of agitating or the state of being agitated.
2. Extreme emotional disturbance; perturbation

are intransigent[94] to recognize the **doctrine of equality** in matters of public employment and who under the mistaken impression that 'wrinkles and gray hairs' could not do any thing in this matter, actively participated in the agitation. Similarly, another section of people suffering from a fear psychosis that the Mandal recommendations may not at all be implemented entered the fray of the agitation. Thus, both the pro and anti-reservation on being detonated and inflamed by the ruffled feelings that their future in public employment is bleak raised a number of gnawing[95] doubts which in turn sensationalized the issue. Their pent up fury led to an orgy of violence resulting in loss of innocent life and damaged the public properties. It is heart-rending that some youths - particularly students - in their prime of life went to the extent of even self-immolating themselves. No denying the fact that the horrible, spine - chilling and jarring piece of information that some youths whose feelings ran high had put an end to their lives in tragic and pathetic manner had really caused a tremor in Indian society.

Concept of Equality:

Part-III of Constitution dealing with 'Fundamental Rights'[96] and Part-IV dealing with 'Directive Principles of State Policy'[97] represent the core of the Indian Constitutional philosophy envisage the methodology for removal of historic injustice and inequalities -either inherited or artificially created - and social and economic disparity and ultimately for achieving an egalitarian society in terms of the basic structure of our Constitution as spelt out by the preamble[98].

94 **Meaning of Intransigent:** Refusing to moderate a position, especially an extreme position; uncompromising.

95 **Meaning of Gnawing:**
    a. To bite, chew on, or erode with the teeth.
    b. To erode or diminish gradually as if by gnawing

96 **Meaning of Fundamental Rights:** The Fundamental Rights are defined as basic human freedoms which every Indian citizen has the right to enjoy for a proper and harmonious development of personality. These rights universally apply to all citizens, irrespective of race, place of birth, religion, caste, creed, colour or gender. Aliens (persons who are not citizens) are also considered in matters like equality before law. They are enforceable by the courts, subject to certain restrictions

97 The **Directive Principles of State Policy** are guidelines to the central and state governments of India, to be kept in mind while framing laws and policies. These provisions, contained in Part IV of the Constitution of India, are not enforceable by any court, but the principles laid down therein are considered fundamental in the governance of the country, making it the duty of the State[1] to apply these principles in making laws to establish a just society in the country.

98 A **preamble** is an introductory and expressionary statement in a document that

Though all men and women created by the Almighty, whether orthodox[99] or heterodox[100]; whether theist[101] or atheist[102]; whether born in the highest class or lowest class; whether belong to 'A' religion or 'B' religion are biologically same, having same purity of blood. In a Hindu Society they are divided into a number of distinct sections and sub sections known as castes and sub castes. The moment a child comes out of the mother's womb in a Hindu family and takes its first breath and even before its umbilical cord is cut off, the innocent child is branded, stigmatized and put in a separate slot according to the caste of its parents despite the fact that the birth of the child in the particular slot is not by choice but by chance. The concept of inequality is unknown in the kingdom of God who creates all beings equal, but the "created" of the creator has created the artificial inequality in the name of casteism with selfish motive and vested interest.

Swami Vivekananda in one of his letters addressed to his disciples[103] in Madras dated 24.1.1894 has stated thus:

Caste or no caste, creed or no creed, or class, or caste, or nation, or institution which bars the power of free thought and action of an individual - even so long as that power does not injure others - is devilish[104] and must go down[105].

The Hindus who form the majority, in our country, are divided into 4 Varnas - namely, Brahmins, Kshatriyas, Vaishyas (who are all twice born) and lastly Shudras. Shudras are recognised as being the lowest rung of the hierarchical race. This system not only creates extreme forms of caste and

---

explains the document's purpose and underlying philosophy. When applied to the opening paragraphs of a statute, it may recite historical facts pertinent to the subject of the statute. It is distinct from the long title or enacting formula of a law.

99 **Meaning of Orthodox:** Adhering to the accepted or traditional and established faith, especially in religion

100 **Meaning of Heterodox:**
   1. Not in agreement with accepted beliefs, especially in church doctrine or dogma.
   2. Holding unorthodox opinions

101 **Meaning of Theist:** A person who believes in the existence of God

102 **Meaning of Atheist:** One who disbelieves or denies the existence of God or gods

103 **Meaning of Disciple:** One who embraces and assists in spreading the teachings of another.

104 **Meaning of Devilish:** of, resembling, or characteristic of a devil, as:
   a. Malicious; evil.
   b. Mischievous, teasing, or annoying

105 Vide 'The Complete Works of Swami Vivekananda, Vol. V page 29'

gender prejudices, injustices, inequalities but also divides the society into privileged and disabled, revered and despised and so on. The perpetuation of casteism, in the words of Swami Vivekananda "continues social tyranny of ages". The caste system has been religiously preserved in many ways including by the judicial verdicts, pronounced according to the traditional Hindu Law.

There are various Constitutional provisions such as Articles 14, 15, 16, 17[106], 38[107], 46[108], 332[109],

---

106 **Article 17 in The Constitution Of India 1949**
17. Abolition of Untouchability: Untouchability is abolished and its practice in any form is forbidden The enforcement of any disability arising out of Untouchability shall be an offence punishable in accordance with law

107 **Article 38 in The Constitution Of India 1949**
38. State to secure a social order for the promotion of welfare of the people
(1) The State shall strive to promote the welfare of the people by securing and protecting as effectively as it may a social order in which justice, social, economic and political, shall inform all the institutions of the national life
(2) The State shall, in particular, strive to minimize the inequalities in income, and endeavor to eliminate inequalities in status, facilities and opportunities, not only amongst individuals but also amongst groups of people residing in different areas or engaged in different vocations

108 **Article 46 in The Constitution Of India 1949**
46. Promotion of educational and economic interests of Scheduled Castes, Scheduled Tribes and other weaker sections: The State shall promote with special care the educational and economic interests of the weaker sections of the people, and, in particular, of the Scheduled Castes and the Scheduled Tribes, and shall protect them from social injustice and all forms of exploitation

109 **Article 332 in The Constitution Of India 1949**
332. Reservation of seats for Scheduled Castes and Scheduled Tribes in the Legislative Assemblies of the States
(1) Seats shall be reserved for the Scheduled Castes and the Scheduled Tribes, except the Scheduled Tribes in the tribal areas of Assam, in Nagaland and in Meghalaya, in the Legislative Assembly of every State
(2) Seats shall be reserved also for the autonomous districts in the Legislative Assembly of the State of Assam
(3) The number of seats reserved for the Scheduled Castes or the Scheduled Tribes in the Legislative Assembly nearly as may be, the same proportion to the total number of seats in the Assembly as the population of the Scheduled Castes in th State or of the Scheduled Tribes in the State or part of the State, as the case may be, in respect of which seats are so reserved bears to the total population of the State
(4) The number of seats reserved for an autonomous district in the legislative Assembly of the State of Assam shall bear to the total number of seats in that Assembly a proportion not less than the population of the district bears to the total population of the State
(5) The constituencies for the seats reserved for any autonomous district of Assam shall not comprise any area outside that district

335^{110}, 338^{111} and 340^{112} which are designed to redress the centuries old grievances of the scheduled castes and scheduled tribes as well as the backward classes and which have come for judicial interpretation on and off. It is not merely a part of the Constitution but also a national commitment.

For providing reservations for backward class of citizens, Scheduled Castes and Scheduled Tribes in the public educational institutions and for

---

(6) No person who is not a member of a Scheduled Tribe of any autonomous district of the State of Assam shall be eligible for election to the Legislative Assembly of the State from any constituency of that district

110 **Article 335 in The Constitution Of India 1949**
335. Claims of Scheduled Castes and Scheduled Tribes to services and posts: The claims of the members of the Scheduled Castes and the Scheduled Tribes shall be taken into consideration, consistently with the maintenance of efficiency of administration, in the making of appointments to services and posts in connection with the affairs of the Union or of a State

111 **Article 338 in The Constitution Of India 1949**
338. Special Officer for Scheduled Castes, Scheduled Tribes etc
(1) There shall be a Special Officer for the Scheduled Castes and Scheduled Tribes to be appointed by the President
(2) It shall be the duty of the Special Officer to investigate all matters relating to the safeguards provided for the Scheduled Castes and Scheduled Tribes under this Constitution and report to the President upon the working of those safeguards at such intervals as the President may direct, and the President shall cause all such reports to be laid before each House of Parliament
(3) In this article references to the Scheduled Castes and Scheduled Tribes shall be construed as including references to such other backward classes as the President may, on receipt of the report of a Commission appointed under clause (1) of Article 340, by order specify and also to the Anglo Indian community

112 **Article 340 in The Constitution Of India 1949**
340. Appointment of a Commission to investigate the conditions of backward classes
(1) The President may by order appoint a Commission consisting of such persons as he thinks fit to investigate the conditions of socially and educationally backward classes within the territory of India and the difficulties under which they labour and to make recommendations as to the steps that should be taken by the Union or any State to remove such difficulties and to improve their condition and as to the grants that should be made for the purpose by the Union or any State the conditions subject to which such grants should be made, and the order appointing such Commission shall define the procedure to be followed by the Commission
(2) A Commission so appointed shall investigate the matters referred to them and present to the President a report setting out the facts as found by them and making such recommendations as they think proper
(3) The President shall cause a copy of the report so presented together with a memorandum explaining the action taken thereon to be laid before each House of Parliament

providing equal opportunity in the matters of public employment, some States have appointed Commissions on Backward Classes. The Central Government has also appointed two Commissions under Article 340(1) of the Constitution of India for identifying the backward class of citizens as contemplated under Article 16(4) for the purpose of making reservation of appointments or posts in the Services under Union of India.

Second Backward Classes Commission (popularly known as Mandal Commission)

By a Presidential Order under Article 340 of the Constitution of India, the first Backward Class Commission known as Kaka Kalelkar's Commission was set up on January 29, 1953 and it submitted its report on March 30, 1955 listing out 2399 castes as socially and educationally backward on the basis of criteria evolved by it, but the Central Government did not accept that report and shelved it in the cold storage.

It was about twenty-four years after the First Backward Classes Commission submitted its Report in 1955 that the President of India pursuant to the resolution of the Parliament appointed the second Backward Classes Commission on 1st January 1979 under the Chairmanship of Shri B.P. Mandal to investigate the conditions of **Socially and Educationally Backward Classes (for short 'SEBCs')** within the territory of India. One of the terms of reference of the Commission was to determine the criteria for defining the SEBCs. The Commission commenced its functioning on 21st March 1979 and completed its work on 12th December 1980, during the course of which it made an extensive tour throughout the length and breadth of India in order to collect the requisite data for its final report. The Commission submitted its report on 31st December 1980. The Commission appears to have identified as many as 3743 castes as SEBCs and made its recommendations under Chapter XIII of Volume I of its report[113] and finally suggested "regarding the period of operation of Commission's recommendations, the entire scheme should be reviewed after twenty years[114].

Government after having carefully considering the report and the recommendations of the Commission, issued following orders:

(i) 27% of the vacancies in civil posts and services under the Government of India shall be reserved for SEBC.

113 (vide paras 13.1 to 13.39)

114 (Vide para 13.40)

(ii) The aforesaid reservation shall apply to vacancies to be filled by direct recruitment.

(iii) Candidates belonging to SEBC recruited on the basis of merit in an open competition on the same standards prescribed for the general candidates shall not be adjusted against the reservation quota of 27%.

(iv) The SEBC would comprise in the first phase the castes and communities which are common to both the list in the report of the Mandal Commission and the State Governments' lists.

(v) The aforesaid reservation shall take effect from 7.8.1990.

Question before the Supreme Court:

A. Whether "class" in Article 16(4) of the Constitution means "caste"? Can caste be adopted as a collectivity to identify the backward classes for the purposes of Article16(4)?

B. Whether the expression "any backward class of citizens" in Article 16(4) means "socially and educationally backward classes" as it is in Article 15(4)?

C. What is meant by the expression "any backward class of citizens not adequately represented in the Services under the State" in Article 16(4)?

D. Whether Article 16(4) permits reservation of appointments or posts at the stage of initial entry into Government Services or even in the process of promotion?

E. Whether Article 16(4) is exhaustive of the State-power to provide job-reservations?

F. To what extent reservations are permissible under Article 16(4)? Below 50% or to any extent?

G. Can poverty be the sole criterion for identifying the "backward class" under Article16(4).

Legislative History of Article 15(4) of the Constitution

A legislative historical event that warranted the introduction of Clause 4 to Article 15 may be briefly retraced. The Government of Tamil Nadu issued a Communal G.O. in 1927 making compartmental reservation of posts for various communities. Subsequently the G.O. was revised. In

1950 one Smt. Champakam Dorairajan who intended to join the Medical College, on enquiries came to know that in respect of admissions into the Government Medical College the authorities were enforcing and observing an order of the Government, namely, notification G.O. No. 1254 Education dated 17.5.1948 commonly known as Communal G.O. which restricted the number of seats in Government Colleges for certain castes. It appeared that the proportion fixed in the old Communal G.O. had been adhered to even after commencement of the Constitution on January 26, 1950. She filed a Writ Petition on 7th June 1950 under Article 226[115] of the Constitution for issuance of a writ of mandamus[116] restraining the State of Madras from enforcing the said Communal G.O. on the ground

---

115 **Article 226 in The Constitution Of India 1949**
   226. Power of High Courts to issue certain writs
   (1) Notwithstanding anything in Article 32 every High Court shall have powers, throughout the territories in relation to which it exercise jurisdiction, to issue to any person or authority, including in appropriate cases, any Government, within those territories directions, orders or writs, including writs in the nature of habeas corpus, mandamus, prohibitions, quo warranto and certiorari, or any of them, for the enforcement of any of the rights conferred by Part III and for any other purpose
   (2) The power conferred by clause (1) to issue directions, orders or writs to any Government, authority or person may also be exercised by any High Court exercising jurisdiction in relation to the territories within which the cause of action, wholly or in part, arises for the exercise of such power, notwithstanding that the seat of such Government or authority or the residence of such person is not within those territories
   (3) Where any party against whom an interim order, whether by way of injunction or stay or in any other manner, is made on, or in any proceedings relating to, a petition under clause (1), without
   (a) furnishing to such party copies of such petition and all documents in support of the plea for such interim order; and
   (b) giving such party an opportunity of being heard, makes an application to the High Court for the vacation of such order and furnishes a copy of such application to the party in whose favour such order has been made or the counsel of such party, the High Court shall dispose of the application within a period of two weeks from the date on which it is received or from the date on which the copy of such application is so furnished, whichever is later, or where the High Court is closed on the last day of that period, before the expiry of the next day afterwards on which the High Court is open; and if the application is not so disposed of, the interim order shall, on the expiry of that period, or, as the case may be, the expiry of the aid next day, stand vacated
   (4) The power conferred on a High Court by this article shall not be in derogation of the power conferred on the Supreme court by clause (2) of Article 32

116 **Mandamus** is a judicial remedy in the form of an order from a superior court, to any government subordinate court, corporation, or public authority—to do (or forbear from doing) some specific act which that body is obliged under law to do (or refrain from doing)—and which is in the nature of public duty, and in certain cases one of a statutory duty. It cannot be issued to compel an authority to do something against statutory provision

that the G.O. was sought or purported to be regulated in such a manner as to infringe the violation of the fundamental rights guaranteed under Articles 15(1) and 29(2)[117]. Similarly one Srinivasan who had applied for admission into the Government Engineering College at Guindy also filed a Writ Petition praying for a writ of mandamus for the same relief as in Champakam Dorairajan. A full bench of the Madras High Court heard both the Writ Petitions and allowed them (vide *Smt. Champakam Dorairajan and Anr. v. State of Madras*[118]. While the Writ Petition was pending before the High Court, another revised G.O. No. 2208 dated June 16, 1950 substantially reproducing the communal proportion fixed in the old Communal G.O. came into being. The State on being aggrieved by the judgment of the Madras High Court preferred an appeal[119] before Supreme Court in *State of Madras v. Smt. Champakam Dorairajan*[120]. A seven Judges Bench dismissed the appeal holding that "the Communal G.O. being inconsistent with the provisions of Article 29(2) in Part III[121] of

---

117 **Article 29 in The Constitution Of India 1949**
   29. Protection of interests of minorities
   (1) Any section of the citizens residing in the territory of India or any part thereof having a distinct language, script or culture of its own shall have the right to conserve the same
   (2) No citizen shall be denied admission into any educational institution maintained by the State or receiving aid out of State funds on grounds only of religion, race, caste, language or any of them

118 AIR1951Mad120

119 **Meaning of Appeal:** In law, an **appeal** is a process for requesting a formal change to an official decision. Very broadly speaking there are appeals on the record and *de novo* appeals. In *de novo* appeals, a new decision maker re-hears the case without any reference to the prior decision maker. In appeals on the record, the decision of the prior decision maker is challenged by arguing that he or she misapplied the law, came to an incorrect factual finding, acted in excess of his jurisdiction, abused his powers, was biased, considered evidence which he should not have considered or failed to consider evidence that he should have considered

120 [1951]2SCR525

121 '*Part III – Fundamental Rights*' is a charter of rights contained in the Constitution of India. It guarantees civil liberties such that all Indians can lead their lives in peace and harmony as citizens of India. These include individual rights common to most liberal democracies, such as equality before law, freedom of speech and expression, and peaceful assembly, freedom to practice religion, and the right to constitutional remedies for the protection of civil rights by means of writs such as habeas corpus. Violation of these rights result in punishments as prescribed in the Indian Penal Code or other special laws, subject to discretion of the judiciary. The Fundamental Rights are defined as basic human freedoms which every Indian citizen has the right to enjoy for a proper and harmonious development of personality. These rights universally apply to all citizens, irrespective of race, place of birth, religion, caste or gender. Aliens (persons who are not

the Constitution was void under Article 13[122]" This judgment necessitated the introduction of a Bill called Constitution (First Amendment) Bill for over-riding the decision of Supreme Court in Champakam's case.

During the Parliament Debates held on 29th May 1951 Pt. Jawahar Lal Nehru, the then Prime Minister while moving the Bill to amend the Constitution stated as follows:

We have to deal with the situation where for a variety of causes for which the present generation is not to blame, the past has the responsibility, there are groups, classes, individuals, communities, if you like, who are backward. They are backward in many ways - economically, socially, educationally - sometimes they are not backward in one of these respects and yet backward in another. The fact is, therefore that if we wish to encourage them in regard to these matters, we have to do something special for them....

There one has to keep a balance between the existing fact as we find it and the objective and ideal that we aim at.

Thereafter, the Bill was passed and Clause (4) to Article 15 was added by the Constitution (First Amendment) Act. The object of the newly introduced Clause (4) to Article 15 was to bring Articles 15 and 29 in line with Articles 16(4), 46 and 340 and to make it constitutionally valid for the State to reserve seats for backward class of citizens, scheduled castes and scheduled tribes in the public educational institutions as well as to make

---

citizens) are also considered in matters like equality before law. They are enforceable by the courts, subject to certain restrictions. The Rights have their origins in many sources, including England's Bill of Rights, the United States Bill of Rights and France's Declaration of the Rights of Man

122 **Article 13 in The Constitution Of India 1949**
13. Laws inconsistent with or in derogation of the fundamental rights
(1) All laws in force in the territory of India immediately before the commencement of this Constitution, in so far as they are inconsistent with the provisions of this Part, shall, to the extent of such inconsistency, be void
(2) The State shall not make any law which takes away or abridges the rights conferred by this Part and any law made in contravention of this clause shall, to the extent of the contravention, be void
(3) In this article, unless the context otherwise requires law includes any Ordinance, order, bye law, rule, regulation, notification, custom or usages having in the territory of India the force of law; laws in force includes laws passed or made by Legislature or other competent authority in the territory of India before the commencement of this Constitution and not previously repealed, notwithstanding that any such law or any part thereof may not be then in operation either at all or in particular areas
(4) Nothing in this article shall apply to any amendment of this Constitution made under Article 368 Right of Equality

other special provisions as may be necessary for their advancement.

Scope of Article 16(4) of the Constitution

Article 16(4) expressly permits the State to make any provision for the reservation of appointments or posts in favour of any backward class of citizens which in the opinion of the State are not adequately represented in the services under the State. As the power conferred on the State under this Clause 4 is to be exercised only if 'in the opinion of the State' that there is no adequate representation in the services under the State, a vital question arose for consideration whether the issue of determination by the State as to whether a particular class of citizens is backward or not is a justiciable one? This question was answered by the Constitution Bench of Supreme Court in *Trilok Nath Tiku and Anr. v. State of Jammu & Kashmir and Ors.*[123] holding thus:

While the State has necessarily to ascertain whether a particular class of citizens are backward or not, having regard to acceptable criteria, it is not the final word on the question; it is a justiciable[124] issue. While ordinarily a Court may accept the decision of the State in that regard, it is open to be canvassed if that decision is based on irrelevant considerations. The power under Clause (4) is also conditioned by the fact that in regard to any backward classes of citizens there is no adequate representation in the services under the State. The opinion of the State in this regard may ordinarily be accepted as final, except when it is established that there is an abuse of power. The words ' "backward class of citizens" occurring in Article 16(4) are neither defined nor explained in the Constitution though the same words occurring in Article 15(4) are followed by a qualifying phrase, "Socially and Educationally".

Meaning of Backward

The word 'backward' is very wide bringing within its fold the social backwardness, educational backwardness, economic backwardness, political backwardness and even physical backwardness. The meaning of the word 'backward' is defined in lexicons as 'retarded in physical, material or intellectual development' or 'slow in growth or development; retarded".

---

123 (1967)IILLJ271SC

124 **Meaning of Justiciable:** Capable of being determined by a court of law

Meaning of 'Class' and 'Caste'

Caste-system in India is sui-generis[125] to Hindu religion. The Hindu-orthodoxy believes that an early hymn in the Rigveda (the Purusasukta:-10.90) and the much later Manava Dharma Sastra (law of Manu), are the sources of the caste-system. Manu, the law-giver cites the Purusasukta as the source and justification for the caste division of his own time. Among the Aryans the priestly caste was called the Brahmans, the warriors were called the kshatriyas, the common people divided to agriculture, pastoral pursuits, trade and industry were called the Vaishyas and the Dasas or non-Aryans and people of mix-blood were assigned the status of Shudras. The Chaturvama- system has been gradually distorted in shape and meaning and has been replaced by the prevalent caste-system in Hindu society. The caste system kept a large section of people in this country outside the fold of the society who were called the untouchables. Manu required that the dwellings of the untouchables shall be outside the village-their dress, the garments of the dead-their food given to them in a broken dish. The Framers of the Constitution have given a special place to the erstwhile untouchables under the Constitution. The so called untouchable-castes have been named as Scheduled Castes and Scheduled Tribes and for them reservations and other benefits have been provided under the Constitution. Even now if a Hindu-caste stakes its claim as high as that of Scheduled Castes it can be included in that category by following the procedure under the Constitution.

The caste system as projected by Manu and accepted by the Hindu society has proved to be the biggest curse for this country. The Chaturvarna-system under the Aryans was more of an occupational order projecting the division of labour. Thereafter, in the words of Professor Harold A. Gould in his book "The Hindu Caste System", the Brahmins "sacralized the occupational order, and occupationalised the sacred order". With the passage of time the caste-system became the cancer-cell of the Hindu Society.

Before the invasions of the Turks and establishment of Muslim rule the caste-system had brought havoc to the social order. The Kshtriyas being the only fighters, three fourth of the Hindu society was a mute witness to the plunder of the country by the foreigners. Mahmud Ghazni raided and looted India for seventeen times during 1000 AD to 1027 AD. In 1025 AD Mahmud Ghazni raided the famous temple of Somanath. Thereafter between 1175 AD and 1195 AD Mahmud Ghazni invaded India several

---

125 **Sui generis** is a Latin phrase, meaning "of its own kind/genus" and hence "unique in its characteristics"

times. *According to the historians one of the causes of the defeat of the Indians at the hands of Turks was the prevalent social conditions especially the caste system of Hindus.*

This country remained under shackles of slavery for over one thousand years. The reason for our inability to fight the foreign-rule was the social de-generation of India because of the caste-system. To rule this country it was not necessary to divide the people, the caste-system conveyed the message "Divided we are - come and rule us".

It was only in the later part of 19th century that the national movement took birth in this country. With the advent of the 20th century Mahatma Gandhi, Jawahar Lal Nehru alongwith other leaders infused national and secular spirit amongst the people of India. For the first time in the history of India caste, creed and religion were forgotten and people came together under one banner to fight the British rule. The caste-system was thrown to the winds and people from all walks of life marched together under the slogan of 'Quit-India'. It was not the Kshatriyas alone who were the freedom fighters - whole of the country fought for freedom. It was the unity and the integrity of the people of India which brought freedom to them after thousand years of slavery. The Constitution of India was drafted in the background of the freedom struggle. Secularism[126] is the basic feature of the Indian Constitution. It envisages a cohesive, unified and casteless society. The Constitution has completely obliterated the caste-system and has assured equality before law.

In Webster Comprehensive Dictionary (International Edition), the meaning of the words is given as follows:

Class

A number or body of persons with common characteristics: the educated class

Caste

One of the hereditary classes into which Hindu society is divided in India

---

126 **Secularism** is the principle of the separation of government institutions and persons mandated to represent the state from religious institutions and religious dignitaries. One manifestation of secularism is asserting the right to be free from religious rule and teachings, or, in a state declared to be neutral on matters of belief, from the imposition by government of religion or religious practices upon its people. Another manifestation of secularism is the view that public activities and decisions, especially political ones, should remain uninfluenced by religious beliefs and/ or practices

According to Webster's Encyclopedic Unabridged Dictionary of the English Language, meaning of the words 'class' and 'caste' is as follows:

Class

(1) a number of persons or things regarded as forming a group by reason of common attributes, characteristics, qualities, or traits, kind, sort (2) any division of persons or things according to rank or grade

Caste

(1) Social, an endogamous[127] and hereditary social group limited to persons of the same rank, occupation, economic position etc. and having mores distinguishing it from other such groups, (2) any rigid system of social distinctions (2) Hinduism, any of the four social divisions, the Brahman, Kshatriya, Vaisya and Sudra, into which Hindu society is rigidly divided, each caste having its own privileges and limitations, transferred by inheritance from one generation to the next (3) any class or group of society sharing common cultural features.

Whether Article 16(4) contemplates reservation in the matter of promotion?

In *Mohan Kumar Singhania V. Union of India*[128], a three-Judges Bench of Supreme Court has taken a view that once candidates even from reserved communities are allocated and appointed to a Service based on their ranks and performance and brought under the one and same stream of category, then they too have to be treated on par with all other selected candidates and there cannot be any question of preferential treatment at that stage on the ground that they belong to reserved community though they may be entitled for all other statutory benefits such as the relaxation of age, the reservation etc. Reservation referred to in that context is referable to the *reservation at the initial stage or the entry point as could be gathered from that judgment.*

Article 16(4) does not permit provision for reservation in the matter of promotions and that this rule shall, however, have only prospective operation and shall not affect the promotions already made, whether made on regular basis or on any other basis.

---

127 **Meaning of Endogamous**: Pertaining to or characterized by the custom of marrying only within the limits of a clan or tribe

128 AIR1992SC1

Decision by Supreme Court

1) Article 16(4) of the Constitution is neither an exception nor a proviso to Article16(1). It is exhaustive of all the reservations that can be made in favour of backward class of citizens. It has an over-riding effect on Article 16(1) and (2).

2) No Reservation can be made under Article 16(4) for classes other than backward classes. But under Article 16(1), reservation can be made for classes, not covered by Article 16(4).

3) The expression, 'backward class of citizens' occurring in Article 16(4) is neither defined nor explained in the Constitution. However, the backward class or classes can certainly be identified in Hindu society with reference to castes along with other criteria such as traditional occupation, poverty, place of residence, lack of education etc. and in communities where caste is not recognised by the above recognised and accepted criteria except caste criterion.

4) In the process of identification of backward class of citizens under Article 16(4)among Hindus, caste is a primary criterion or a dominant factor though it is not the sole criterion.

5) Any provision under Article 16(4) is not necessarily to be made by the Parliament or Legislature. Such a provision could also be made by an Executive order.

6) The power conferred on the State under Article 16(4) is one coupled with a duty and, therefore, the State has to exercise that power for the benefit of all those, namely, backward class for whom it is intended.

7) The provision for reservation of appointments or posts in favour of any backward class of citizens is a matter of policy of the Government, of course subject to the constitutional parameters and well settled principles of judicial review[129].

8) No maximum ceiling of reservation can be fixed under Article 16(4) of the Constitution for reservation of appointments or posts in favour of any backward class of citizens "in the Services under the State". The decisions fixing the percentage of reservation only up to the maximum of 50% are unsustainable.

9) No section of the SEBCs can be excluded on the ground of creamy layer

---

129 **Meaning of Judicial Review**: The power of a court to adjudicate the constitutionality of legislative or executive acts

till the Government - Central and State - takes a decision in this regard on a review on the recommendations of a Commission or a Committee to be appointed by the Government.

10) The Government of India and the State Governments have to create a permanent machinery either by way of a Commission or a Committee within a reasonable time for examining the requests of inclusion or exclusion of any caste, community or group of persons on the advice of such Commission or Committee, as the case may be, and also for examining the exclusion of any pseudo[130] community if smuggled into the list of OBCs.

11) The Constitution prohibits discrimination on grounds only of religion, race, caste, sex, descent, place of birth, residence or any of them. Any discrimination solely on any one or more of these prohibited grounds will result in invidious reverse discrimination which is impermissible. None of these grounds is the sole or the dominant or the indispensable criterion to identify backwardness which qualifies for reservation. But each of them is, in conjunction with factors such as poverty, illiteracy, demeaning occupation, malnutrition, physical and intellectual deformity and like disadvantages, a relevant criterion to identify socially and educationally backward classes of citizens for whom reservation is intended.

12) Reservation contemplated under Article 16 is meant exclusively for backward classes of citizens who are not adequately represented in the services under the State.

13) Only such classes of citizens who are socially and educationally backward are qualified to be identified as backward classes. To be accepted as backward classes for the purpose of reservation under Article 15 or Article 16, their backwardness must have been either recognised by means of a notification by the President under Article341[131] or Article 342[132] declaring them to be

---

130 **Meaning of Pseudo**: False or counterfeit; fake

131 **Article 341 in The Constitution Of India 1949**
341. Scheduled Castes
> (1) The President may with respect to any State or Union territory, and where it is a State after consultation with the Governor thereof, by public notification, specify the castes, races or tribes or parts of or groups within castes, races or tribes which shall for the purposes of this Constitution be deemed to be Scheduled Castes in relation to that State or Union territory, as the case may be
> (2) Parliament may by law include in or exclude from the list of Scheduled Castes specified in a notification issued under clause (1) any caste, race or tribe or part of or group within any caste, race or tribe, but save as aforesaid a notification issued under the said clause shall not be varied by any subsequent notification

132 **Article 342 in The Constitution Of India 1949**

Scheduled Castes or Scheduled Tribes, or, on an objective consideration, identified by the State to be socially and educationally so backward by reason of identified prior discrimination and its continuing ill effects as to be comparable to the Scheduled Castes or the Scheduled Tribes.

14) Members of the Scheduled Castes or the Scheduled Tribes do not lose the benefits of reservation and other affirmative action programmes intended for backward classes merely by reason of their conversion from the Hindu or the Sikh or the Buddhist religion to any other religion, and all such persons shall continue to be accorded all such benefits until such time as they cease to be backward.

15) Once a class of citizens is identified on correct principles as backward for the purpose of reservation, the "means test" must be strictly and uniformly applied to exclude all those persons in that class reaching above the predetermined economic level.

16) Reservation in all cases must be confined to a minority of available posts or seats so as not to unduly sacrifice merits. The number of seats or posts reserved under Article 15 or Article 16 must at all times remain well below 50% of the total number of seats or posts.

17) Reservation has no application to promotion. It is confined to initial appointment, whichever be the level or grade a which such appointment is made in the administrative hierarchy, and whether or not the post in question is borne on the cadre of the service.

18) Once reservation is strictly confined to the constitutionally intended beneficiaries, as aforesaid, there will probably be no need to disappoint any deserving candidate legitimately seeking the benefit of reservation, for there will then be sufficient room well within the 50% limit for ail candidates belonging to the backward classes as properly determined on correct principles. In that event, questions such as caste or religion will become merely academic and the competing maddening rush for

---

342. Scheduled Tribes

(1) The President may with respect to any State or Union territory, and where it is a State, after consultation with the Governor thereof, by public notification, specify the tribes or tribal communities or parts of or groups within tribes or tribal communities which shall for the purposes of this Constitution be deemed to be Scheduled Tribes in relation to that State or Union territory, as the case may be

(2) Parliament may by law include in or exclude from the list of Scheduled Tribes specified in a notification issued under clause (1) any tribe or tribal community or part of or group within any tribe or tribal community, but save as aforesaid a notification issued under the said clause shall not be varied by any subsequent notification

"backward" label will vanish.

19) A periodic administrative review of all affirmative action programmes, including reservation of seats or posts, must be conducted by a specially constituted Permanent Authority with a view to adjustment and readjustment of such programmes in proportion to the nature, degree and extent of backwardness. All such programmes must stand the test of judicial review whenever challenged. Reservation being exclusionary in character must necessarily stand the test of heightened administrative and judicial solicitude so as to be confined to the strict bounds of constitutional principles.

20) Poverty demands affirmative action. Its eradication is a constitutional mandate. The immediate target to which every affirmative action programme contemplated by Article 15 or Article 16 is addressed is poverty causing backwardness. But it is only such poverty which is the continuing ill-effect of identified prior discrimination, resulting in backwardness comparable to that of the Scheduled Castes or the Scheduled Tribes, that justifies reservation.

21) In the final analysis, poverty which is the ultimate result of inequities and which is the immediate cause and effect of backwardness has to be eradicated not merely by reservation as aforesaid, but by free medical aid, free elementary education, scholarships for higher education and other financial support, free housing, self- employment and settlement schemes, effective implementation of land reforms, strict and impartial operation of the law-enforcing machinery, industrialisation, construction of roads, bridges, culverts, canals, markets, introduction of transport, free supply of water, electricity and other ameliorative measures particularly in areas densely populated by backward classes of citizens.

Conclusion:

A. Reservation of seats or posts for backward classes of citizens, including those for the Scheduled Castes and the Scheduled Tribes, must remain well below 50% of the total seats or posts.

B. Reservation is confined to initial appointment to a post and has no application to promotion.

Chapter-8

Right of Minorities to Establish and Administer Educational Institutions of their choice[133]

Facts in Nutshell

India is a land of diversity -- of different castes, peoples, communities, languages, religions and culture. Although these people enjoy complete political freedom, a vast part of the multitude is illiterate and lives below the poverty line. The single most powerful tool for the upliftment and progress of such diverse communities is deduction. The state, with its limited resources and slow-moving machinery, is unable to fully develop the genius of the Indian people very often the impersonal education that is imparted by the state, devoid of adequate material content that will make the students self-reliant only succeeds in producing potential pen-pushers, as a result of which sufficient jobs are not available.

It is in this scenario where there is a lack of quality education and adequate number of schools and colleges that private educational institutions have been established by educationists, philanthropists and religious and linguistic minorities. Their grievance is that the necessary and unproductive load on their back in the form of governmental control, by way of rules and regulations, has thwarted the progress of quality education. It was their contention that the government must get off their back, and that they should be allowed to provide quality education uninterrupted by

---

133 Appellants: T.M.A. Pai Foundation and Ors. Vs. Respondent: State of Karnataka and Ors.
   Hon'ble Judges/Coram: B.N. Kirpal, C.J., G.B. Pattanaik, S. Rajendra Babu, K.G. Balakrishnan, P. Venkatarama Reddi, Dr. Arijit Pasayat, V.N. Khare, S.S.M. Quadri, Ruma Pal, S.N. Variava and Ashok Bhan, JJ.
   Decided On: 31.10.2002, MANU/SC/0905/2002
   Subject: Constitution Law

unnecessary rules and regulations, laid down by the bureaucracy for its own self-importance. The private educational institutions, both aided and unaided, established by minorities and non-minorities, in their desire to break free of the unnecessary shackles put on their functioning as modern educational institutions and seeking to impart quality education for the benefit of the community for whom they were established, and others, filed the writ petitions[134] and appeals[135] asserting their right to establish and administer educational institutions of their choice unhampered by rules and regulations that unnecessarily impinge upon their autonomy.

Writ Petition No. 350 of 1993 filed by the Islamic Academy of Education and connected petitions were placed before a Bench of 5 Judges. As the Bench was prima facie of the opinion that Article 30[136] did not clothe[137] a minority educational institution with the power to adopt its own method of selection and the correctness of the decision of Supreme Court in St. Stephen's College v. University of Delhi, AIR1992SC1630 was doubted, it was directed that the questions that arose should be authoritatively answered by a larger Bench. These cases were then placed before a Bench of 7 Judges. The questions framed were recast and on 6th February, 1997, the Court directed that the matter be placed a Bench of at least 11

---

134 Writ Petition is an order by a higher court to the lower court or courts directing them to act or stop them from doing the activity. The Indian Constitution provides for five writ petition types - Habeas Corpus, Mandamus, Prohibition, Certiorari, Prohibition and Quo Warranto.

135 **Meaning of appeal:**
   a. A higher court's review of the correctness of a decision by a lower court.
   b. A case so reviewed.

136 **Article 30 in The Constitution Of India 1949**
   30. Right of minorities to establish and administer educational institutions
   (1) All minorities, whether based on religion or language, shall have the right to establish and administer educational institutions of their choice
   (1A) In making any law providing for the compulsory acquisition of any property of an educational institution established and administered by a minority, referred to in clause (1), the State shall ensure that the amount fixed by or determined under such law for the acquisition of such property is such as would not restrict or abrogate the right guaranteed under that clause
   (2) The state shall not, in granting aid to educational institutions, discriminate against any educational institution on the ground that it is under the management of a minority, whether based on religion or language

137 **Meaning of clothe:**
   To cover as if with clothing

Judges, as it was felt that in view of the Forty-Second Amendment[138] to the Constitution, whereby "education" had been included in Entry 25 of List III of the Seventh Schedule, the question of who would be regarded as a "minority" was required to be considered because the earlier case laws related to the pre-amendment era, when education was only in the State List.

Contention by the learned counsel for the appellants:

On behalf of all these institutions, the learned counsels have submitted that the Constitution provides a fundamental right to establish and administer educational institutions. With regard to non-minorities, the right was stated to be contained in Article 19(1)(g)[139] and/or

---

138 The 42nd amendment to Constitution of India, officially known as **The Constitution (Forty-second amendment) Act, 1976,** was enacted during the Emergency (25 June 1975 – 21 March 1977) by the Indian National Congress government headed by Indira Gandhi. Most provisions of the amendment came into effect on 3 January 1977, others were enforced from 1 February and Section 27 came into force on 1 April 1977. The 42nd Amendment is regarded as the most controversial constitutional amendment in Indian history. It attempted to reduce the power of the Supreme Court and High Courts to pronounce upon the constitutional validity of laws. It laid down the Fundamental Duties of Indian citizens to the nation.

139 **Article 19 in The Constitution Of India 1949**
19. Protection of certain rights regarding freedom of speech etc
(1) All citizens shall have the right
(a) to freedom of speech and expression;
(b) to assemble peaceably and without arms;
(c) to form associations or unions;
(d) to move freely throughout the territory of India;
(e) to reside and settle in any part of the territory of India; and
(f) omitted
(g) to practise any profession, or to carry on any occupation, trade or business
(2) Nothing in sub clause (a) of clause (1) shall affect the operation of any existing law, or prevent the State from making any law, in so far as such law imposes reasonable restrictions on the exercise of the right conferred by the said sub clause in the interests of the sovereignty and integrity of India, the security of the State, friendly relations with foreign States, public order, decency or morality or in relation to contempt of court, defamation or incitement to an offence
(3) Nothing in sub clause (b) of the said clause shall affect the operation of any existing law in so far as it imposes, or prevent the State from making any law imposing, in the interests of the sovereignty and integrity of India or public order, reasonable restrictions on the exercise of the right conferred by the said sub clause
(4) Nothing in sub clause (c) of the said clause shall affect the operation of any existing law in so far as it imposes, or prevent the State from making any law imposing, in the interests of the sovereignty and integrity of India or public order or morality, reasonable restrictions on the exercise of the right conferred by the said sub clause
(5) Nothing in sub clauses (d) and (e) of the said clause shall affect the operation of any

Article 26[140], while in the case of linguistic and religious minorities, the submission was that this right was enshrined and protected by Article 30. It was further their case that private educational institutions should have full autonomy in their administration. While it is necessary for an educational institution to secure recognition or affiliation, and for which purpose rules and regulations or conditions could be prescribed pertaining to the requirement of the quality of education to be provided, e.g., qualifications of teachers, curriculum to be taught and the minimum facilities which should be available for the students, it was submitted that the state should not have a right to interfere or lay down conditions with regard to the administration of those institutions. In particular, objection was taken to the nominations by the state on the governing bodies of the private institutions, as well as to provisions with regard to the manner of admitting students, the fixing of the fee structure and recruitment of teachers through state channels.

The counsels for the educational institutions, urged that the decision of Supreme Court in *Unni Krishnan, J.P. and Ors. v. State of Andhra Pradesh and Ors.,* [1993]1SCR594 case required reconsideration. It was submitted that the scheme that had been framed in Unni Krishnan's case had imposed unreasonable restrictions on the administration of the private educational institutions, and that especially in the case of minority institutions, the right guaranteed to them under Article 30(1) stood infringed. It was also

---

existing law in so far as it imposes, or prevent the State from making any law imposing, reasonable restrictions on the exercise of any of the rights conferred by the said sub clauses either in the interests of the general public or for the protection of the interests of any Scheduled Tribe

(6) Nothing in sub clause (g) of the said clause shall affect the operation of any existing law in so far as it imposes, or prevent the State from making any law imposing, in the interests of the general public, reasonable restrictions on the exercise of the right conferred by the said sub clause, and, in particular, nothing in the said sub clause shall affect the operation of any existing law in so far as it relates to, or prevent the State from making any law relating to,

(i) the professional or technical qualifications necessary for practising any profession or carrying on any occupation, trade or business, or

(ii) the carrying on by the State, or by a corporation owned or controlled by the State, of any trade, business, industry or service, whether to the exclusion, complete or partial, of citizens or otherwise

140 **Article 26 in The Constitution Of India 1949**

26. Freedom to manage religious affairs Subject to public order, morality and health, every religious denomination or any section thereof shall have the right

(a) to establish and maintain institutions for religious and charitable purposes;

(b) to manage its own affairs in matters of religion;

(c) to own and acquire movable and immovable property; and

(d) to administer such property in accordance with law

urged that the object that was sought to be achieved by the scheme was, in fact, not achieved.

Arguments on behalf of private minority institutions:

On behalf of the private minority institutions, it was submitted that on the correct interpretation of the various provisions of the Constitution, and Articles 29[141] and 30 in particular, the minority institutions have a right to establish and administer educational institutions of their choice. The use of the phrase "of their choice" in Article 30(1) clearly postulated that the religious and linguistic minorities could establish and administer any type of educational institution, whether it was a school, a degree college or a professional college; it was argued that such an educational institution is invariably established primarily for the benefit of the religious and linguistic minority, and it should be open to such institutions to admit students of their choice. While Article 30(2) was meant to ensure that these minority institutions would not be denied aid on the ground that they were managed by minority institutions, it was submitted that no condition which curtailed or took away the minority character of the institution while granting aid could be imposed. In particular, it was submitted that Article 29(2) could not be applied or so interpreted as to completely obliterate the right of the minority institution to grant admission to the students of its own religion or language. It was also submitted that while secular laws relating to health, town planning, etc., would be applicable, no other rules and regulations could be framed that would in any way curtail or interfere with the administration of the minority educational institution. It was emphasized by the learned counsel that the right to administer an educational institution included the right to constitute a governing body, appoint teachers and admit students. It was further submitted that these were the essential ingredients of the administration of an educational institution, and no fetter could be put on the exercise of the right to administer. It was conceded that for the purpose of seeking recognition, qualifications of teachers could be stipulated, as also the qualification of the students who could be admitted; at the same time, it was argued that

---

141 **Article 29 in The Constitution Of India 1949**
   29. Protection of interests of minorities
   (1) Any section of the citizens residing in the territory of India or any part thereof having a distinct language, script or culture of its own shall have the right to conserve the same
   (2) No citizen shall be denied admission into any educational institution maintained by the State or receiving aid out of State funds on grounds only of religion, race, caste, language or any of them

the manner and mode of appointment of teachers and selection of students had to be within the exclusive domain of the autochthones[142] institution.

Arguments on behalf of private non-minority unaided educational institutions:

On behalf of the private non-minority unaided educational institutions, it was contended that since secularism[143] and equality were part of the basic structure of the Constitution the provisions of the Constitution should be interpreted so that the right of the private non-minority unaided institutions were the same as that of the minority institutions. It was submitted that while reasonable restrictions could be imposed under Article 19(6), such private institutions should have the same freedom of administration of an unaided institution as was sought by the minority unaided institutions.

Contention by learned Solicitor General

The learned Solicitor General did not dispute the contention that the right in establish an institution had been confined on the non-minorities by Articles 19 and 26 and on the religious and linguistic minorities by Article 30. He agreed with the submission of the counsels for the appellants that the Unni Krishnan decision required reconsideration, and that the private unaided educational institutions were entitled to greater autonomy. He, however, contended that Article 29(2) was applicable to minority institutions, and the claim of the minority institutions that they could preferably admit students of their own religion or language to the exclusion of the other communities was impermissible. In other words, he submitted that Article 29(2) made it obligatory even on the minority institutions not to deny admission on the ground of religion, race, caste, language or any of them.

Question before the Supreme Court

- *Is there a fundamental right[144] to set up educational institution and*

---

142 **Meaning of autochthones:**
   One that originated or was formed where it is found, especially a rock formation that has not been displaced.

143 **Meaning of secularism:**
   The view that religious considerations should be excluded from civil affairs or public education.

144 Fundamental rights are a group of rights that have been recognized by the Supreme Court as requiring a high degree of protection from government encroachment. These rights are specifically identified in the Constitution.(i.e. in the Bill of Rights), or have

if so, under which provision?

- *Does unnikrishnan's case require reconsideration?*

- *In case of private institutions, can there be government regulations and, if so, to what extent?*

- *In order to determine the existence of a religious or linguistic minority in relation to article 30, what is to be the unit - the state or the country as a whole?*

- *To what extent can the rights of aided private minority institutions to administer be regulated?*

- *Whether Article 30 gives a right to ask for a grant or aid from the state, and secondly, if it does get aid, to examine to what extent its autonomy in* administration, specifically in the matter of admission to the educational institution established by the community, can be curtailed or regulated.

Decision by Supreme Court

Is there a fundamental right to set up educational institution and if so, under which provision

With regard to the establishment of educational institutions, three Articles of the Constitution come into play. Article 19(1)(g) gives the right to all the citizens to practice any profession or to carry on any occupation, trade or business; this right is subject to restrictions that may be placed under Article 19(6). Article 26 gives the right to every religious denomination to establish and maintain an institution for religious purposes, which would include an educational institution. Article 19(1)(g) and Article 26, therefore, confer rights on all citizens and religious denominations to establish and maintain educational institutions. There is no serious dispute that the majority community as well as linguistic and religious minorities would have a right under Article 19(1)(g) and 26 to establish educational institutions. In addition, Article 30(1), in no uncertain terms, gives the right to the religious and linguistic minorities to establish and administer educational institutions of their choice.

Article 19(1)(g) employs four expressions, viz., profession, occupation, trade and business. Their fields may overlap, but each of them does have a content of its own. Education is per se regarded as an activity that is

---

been found under Due Process.

charitable in nature.[145] Education has so far not been regarded as a trade or business where profit is the motive. Even if there is any doubt about whether education is a profession or not, it does appear that education will fall within the meaning of the expression "occupation".

Article 19(1)(g) uses the four expressions so as to cover all activities of a citizen in respect of which income or profit is generated, and which can consequently be regulated under Article 19(6).

In Webster's Third New International Dictionary at page 1650, "occupation" is, inter alia , defined as "an activity in which one engages" or "a craft, trade, profession or other means of earning a living".

In Corpus Juris Secundum, Volume LXVII, the word "occupation" is defined as under:-

"The word "occupation" also is employed as referring to that which occupies time and attention; a calling; or a trade; and it is only as employed in this sense that the word is discussed in the following paragraphs.

There is nothing ambiguous about the word "occupation" as it is used in the sense of employing one's time. It is a relative term, in common use with a well-understand meaning, and very broad in its scope and significance. It is described as a generic and very comprehensive term, which includes every species of the genus, and compasses the incidental, as well as the main, requirements of one's vocation., calling, or business. The word "occupation" is variously defined as meaning the principal business of one's life; the principal or usual business in which a man engages; that which principally takes up one's time, thought, and energies; that which occupies or engages the time and attention; that particular business, profession, trade, or calling which engages the time and efforts of an individual; the employment in which one engages, or the vocation of one's life; the state of being occupied or employed in any way; that activity in which a person, natural or artificial, is engaged with the element of a degree of permanency attached."

A Five Judge Bench in *Sodan Singh and Ors. v. New Delhi* Municipal Committee and Ors., [1989]3SCR1038 at page 174, para 28, observed as follows:

".....The word occupation has a wide meaning such as any regular work, profession, job, principal activity, employment, business or a calling in

---

145 See The State of Bombay v. R.M.D. Chamarbaugwala, MANU/SC/0019/1957

which an individual is engaged.....

The object of using four analogous and overlapping words in Article 19(1)(g) is to make the guaranteed right as comprehensive as possible to include all the avenues and modes through which a man may earn his livelihood. In a nutshell the guarantee takes into its fold any activity carried on by a citizen of India to earn his living....".

In Unni Krishnan's case, at page 687, para 63, while referring to education, it was observed as follows:-

".....It may perhaps fall under the category of occupation provided no recognition is sought from the State or affiliation from the University is asked on the basis that its a fundamental right....."

While the conclusion that "occupation" comprehends the establishment of educational institutions is correct, the proviso in the aforesaid observation to the effect that this is so provided no recognition is sought from the state or affiliation from the concerned university is, with the utmost respect, erroneous. The fundamental right to establish an educational institution cannot be confused with the right to ask for recognition of affiliation. The exercise of a fundamental right may be controlled in a variety of ways. For example, the right to carry on a business does not entail the right to carry on a business at a particular place. The right to carry on a business may be subject to licensing laws so that a denial of the licence presents a person from carrying on that particular business. The question of whether there is a fundamental right or not cannot be dependent upon whether it can be made the subject matter of controls.

The establishment and running of an educational institution where a large number of persons are employed as teachers or administrative staff, and an activity is carried on that results in the imparting of knowledge to the students, must necessarily be regarded as an occupation, even if there is no element of profit generation. It is difficult to comprehended that education, per se, will not fall under any of the four expressions in Article 19(1)(g). "Occupation" would be an activity of a person undertaken as a means of livelihood or a mission in life.

The above quoted observations in Sodan Singh's case correctly interpret the expression "occupation" in Article 19(1)(g).

The right to establish and maintain educational institutions may also be sourced to Article 26(a), which grants, in positive terms, the right to every religious denomination or any section thereof to establish and maintain institutions for religious and charitable purposes, subject to public order, morality and health. Education is a recognized head of charity. therefore, religious denominations or sections thereof, which do not fall within the special categories carved out in Article 29(1) and 30(1), have the right to establish and maintain religious and educational institutions. This would allow members belonging to any religious denomination, including the majority religious community, to set up an educational institution. Given this, the phrase "private educational institution" as used in this judgment would include not only those educational institutions set up by the secular persons or bodies, but also educational institutions set up by religious denominations; the word "private" is used in contradistinction to government institutions.

Does unnikrishnan's case require reconsideration?

In the case of Mohini Jain (Miss) v. State of Karnataka and Ors., [1992]3SCR658 , the challenge was to a notification of June 1989, which provided for a fee structure, whereby for government seats, the tuition fee was Rs. 2, 000 per annum, and for students from Karnataka, the fee was Rs. 25,000 per annum, while the fee for Indian students from outside Karnataka, under the payment category, was Rs. 60,000 per annum. It had been contended that charging such a discriminatory and high fee violated constitutional guarantees and rights. This attack was sustained, and it was held that there was a fundamental right to education in every citizen, and that the state was duty bound to provide the education, and that the private institutions that discharge the state's duties were equally bound not to charge a higher fee than the government institutions. The Court then held that any prescription of fee in excess of what was payable in government colleges was a capitation fee and would, therefore, be illegal. The correctness of this decision was challenged in Unni Krishnan's case, where it was contended that if Mohini Jain's ratio was applied the educational institutions would have to be closed down, as they would be wholly unviable without appropriate funds, by way of tuition fees, from their students.

In Unni Krishnan's case Court considered the conditions and regulations, if any, which the state could impose in the running of private unaided/ aided recognized or affiliated educational institutions conducting professional courses such a medicine, engineering, etc. The extent to which the fee could be charged by such an institution, and the manner in which admissions could be granted was also considered. Supreme Court held that private unaided recognized/affiliated educational institutions running professional courses were entitled to charge a fee higher than that charged by government institutions for similar courses, but that such a fee could not exceed the maximum limit fixed by the state. It held that commercialization of deduction was not permissible, and "was opposed to public policy and Indian tradition and therefore charging capitation fee was illegal." With regard to private aided recognized/affiliated educational institutions, the Court upheld the power of the government to frame rules and regulations in matter of admission and fees, as well as in matters such a recruitment and conditions of service of teachers and staff. Though a question was raised as to whether the setting up of an educational institution could be regarded as a business, profession or vocation under Article 19(1)(g), this question was not answered. Jeevan Reddy, J., however, at page 751, para 197, observed as follows:-

".....While we do not wish to express any opinion on the question whether the right to establish an educational institution can be said to be carrying on any "occupation" within the meaning of Article 19(1)(g), - perhaps, it is -- we are certainly of the opinion that such activity can neither be a trade or business nor can it be a profession within the meaning of Article 19(1) (g). Trade or business normally connotes an activity carried on with a profit motive. Education has never been commerce in this country....."

Reliance was placed on a decision of Supreme Court in Bangalore Water Supply and Sewerage Board v. A. Rajappa and Ors., (1978)ILLJ349SC , wherein it had been held that educational institutions would come within the expression "industry" in the Industrial Disputes Act, and that, therefore, education would come under Article 19(1)(g). But the applicability of this decision was distinguished by Jeevan Reddy, J., observing that "we do not think the said observation (that education as industry) in a different context has any application here". While holding, on an interpretation of Articles 21[146], 41[147], 45[148]

---

146 **Article 21 in The Constitution Of India 1949**
   21. Protection of life and personal liberty No person shall be deprived of his life or personal liberty except according to procedure established by law

147 **Article 41 in The Constitution Of India 1949**
   41. Right to work, to education and to public assistance in certain cases The State shall, within the limits of its economic capacity and development, make effective provision for securing the right to work, to education and to public assistance in cases of unemployment, old age, sickness and disablement, and in other cases of undeserved want

148 **Article 45 in The Constitution Of India 1949**

and 46[149], that a citizen who had not completed the age of 14 years had a right to free education, it was held that such a right was not available to citizens who were beyond the age of 14 years. It was further held that private educational institutions merely supplemented the effort of the state in educating the people. No private educational institution could survive or subsist without recognition and/or affiliation granted by bodies that were the authorities of the state. In such a situation, the Court held that it was obligatory upon the authority granting recognition/affiliation to insist upon such conditions as were appropriate to ensure not only an education of requisite standard, but also fairness and equal treatment in matter of admission of students. The Court then formulated a scheme and directed every authority granting recognition/affiliation to impose that scheme upon institutions seeking recognition/affiliation, even if they were unaided institutions. The scheme that was framed, inter alia, postulated (a) that a professional college should be established and/or administered only by a Society registered under the Societies Registration Act, 1860, or the corresponding Act of a State, or by a Public Trust registered under the Trusts Act, or under the Wakfs Act, and that no individual, firm, company or other body of individuals would be permitted to establish and/or administer a professional college (b) that 50% of the seats in every professional college should be filed by the nominees of the Government or University, selected on the basis of merit determined by a common entrance examination, which will be referred to as "free seats"; the remaining 50% seats ("payment seats") should be filled by those candidates who pay the fee prescribed therefore, and the allotment of students against payment seats should be done on the basis of inter se merit determined on the same basis as in the case of free seats (c) that there should be no quota reserved for the management or for any family, caste or community, which may have established such a college (d) that it should be open to the professional college to provide for reservation of sets for constitutionally permissible classes with the approval of the affiliating university (e) that the fee chargeable in each professional college should be

---

45. Provision for free and compulsory education for children The State shall endeavour to provide, within a period of ten years from the commencement of this Constitution, for free and compulsory education for all children until they complete the age of fourteen years

149 **Article 46 in The Constitution Of India 1949**
46. Promotion of educational and economic interests of Scheduled Castes, Scheduled Tribes and other weaker sections The State shall promote with special care the educational and economic interests of the weaker sections of the people, and, in particular, of the Scheduled Castes and the Scheduled Tribes, and shall protect them from social injustice and all forms of exploitation

subject to such a ceiling as may be prescribed by the appropriate authority or by a competent court (f) that every state government should constitute a committee to fix the ceiling on the fees chargeable by a professional college or class of professional colleges, as the case may be. This committee should, after hearing the professional colleges, fix the fee once every three years or at such longer intervals, as it may think appropriate that it would be appropriate for the University Grants Commission to frame regulators under its Act regulating the fees that the affiliated colleges operating on a no grant-in-aid basis were entitled to charge. The AICTE[150], the Indian Medical Council[151] and the Central Government were also given similar advice. The manner in which the seats to be filled on the basis of the common entrance test was also indicated.

The experience of the educational institutions has been that students who come from private schools, and who belong to more affluent families, are able to secure higher positions in the merit list of the common entrance test, and are thus able to seek admission to the "free seats". Paradoxically, it is the students who come from less affluent families, who are normally able to secure, on the basis of the merit list prepared after the common entrance test, only "payment seats".

The institution thus needs qualified and experienced teachers and proper facilities and equipment, all of which require capital investment. The teachers are required to be paid properly.

The private unaided educational institutions impart education, and that cannot be the reason to take away their choice in matters, inter alia, of selection of students and fixation of fees. Affiliation and recognition has to be available to every institution that fulfills the conditions for grant of such

---

150 **The All India Council for Technical Education (AICTE)** is the statutory body and a national-level council for technical education, under Department of Higher Education, Ministry of Human Resource Development. Established in November 1945 first as an advisory body and later on in 1987 given statutory status by an Act of Parliament, AICTE is responsible for proper planning and coordinated development of the technical education and management education system in India. The AICTE accredits postgraduate and graduate programs under specific categories at Indian institutions as per its charter.

151 **The Medical Council of India (MCI)** Indian Medical Council (Amendment) Ordinance, 2018 (Ordinance 8 of 2018), the Medical Council of India shall stand superseded now is not a statutory body for establishing uniform and high standards of medical education in India. The Council grants recognition of medical qualifications, gives accreditation to medical schools, grants registration to medical practitioners, and monitors medical practice in India.

affiliation and recognition. The private institutions are right in submitting that it is not open to the Court to insist that statutory authorities should impose the terms of the scheme as a condition for grant of affiliation or recognition; this completely destroys the institutional autonomy and the very objective of establishment of the institution.

The Unni Krishnan judgment has created certain problems, and raised thorny issues. In its anxiety to check the commercialization of education, a scheme of "free" and "payment" seats was evolved on the assumption that the economic capacity of first 50% of admitted students would be greater than the remaining 50%, whereas the converse has proved to be the reality. In this scheme, the "payment seat" student would not only pay for his own seat, but also finance the cost of a "free seat" classmate. When one considers the Constitution Bench's earlier statement that higher deduction is not a fundamental right, it seems unreasonable to compel a citizen to pay for the education of another, more so in the unrealistic world of competitive examinations which assess the merit for the purpose of admission solely on the basis of the marks obtained, where the urban students always have an edge over the rural students. In practice, it has been the case of the marginally less merited rural or poor student bearing the burden of a rich and well-exposed urban student.

The scheme in Unni Krishnan's case has the effect of nationalizing education in respect of important features, viz., the right of a private unaided institution to give admission and to fix the fee. By framing this scheme, which has led to the State Governments legislating in conformity with the scheme the private institutions are undistinguishable from the government institutions; curtailing all the essential features of the right of administration of a private unaided educational institution can neither be called fair or reasonable. Even in the decision in Unni Krishnan's case, it has been observed by Jeevan Reddy, J., at page 749, para 194, as follows:

"The hard reality that emerges is that private educational institutions are a necessity in the present day context. It is not possible to do without them because the Governments are in no position to meet the demand - particularly in the sector of medical and technical education which call for substantial outlays. While education is one of the most important functions of the Indian State it has no monopoly therein. Private educational institutions - including minority educational institutions - too have a role to play."

That private educational instructions are a necessity becomes evident from the fact that the number of government-maintained professional colleges has more or less remained stationary, while more private institutions have been established. For example, in the State of Karnataka there are 19 medical colleges out of which there are only 4 government-maintained medical colleges. Similarly, out of 14 Dental Colleges in Karnataka, only one has been established by the government, while in the same State, out of 51 Engineering Colleges, only 12 have been established by the government. The aforesaid figures clearly indicate the important role played by private unaided educational institutions, both minority and non-minority, which cater to the needs of students seeking professional education.

Any system of student selection would be unreasonable if it deprives the private unaided institution of the right of rational selection, which it devised for itself, subject to the minimum qualification that may be prescribed and to some system of computing the equivalence between different kinds of qualifications, like a common entrance test. Such a system of selection can involve both written and oral tests for selection, based on principle of fairness.

Surrendering the total process of selection to the state is unreasonable, as was sought to be done in the Unni Krishnan scheme. Apart from the decision in St. Stephen's College v. University of Delhi, AIR1992SC1630 , which recognized and upheld the right of a minority aided institution to have a rational admission procedure of its own, earlier Constitution Bench decision of this Court have, in effect, upheld such a right of an institution devising a rational manner of selecting and admitting students.

Court hold that the decision in Unni Krishnan's case, insofar as it framed the scheme relating to the grant of admission and the fixing of the fee, was not correct, and to that extent, the said decision and the consequent direction given to UGC, AICTE, Medical Council of India, Central and State Government, etc., are overruled.

In case of private institutions, can there be government regulations and, if so, to what extent?

Private educational institutions, both aided and unaided, are established and administered by religious and linguistic minorities, as well as by non-minorities. Such private educational institutions provide education at three levels, viz., school, college and professional level. It is appropriate to first deal with the case of private unaided institutions and private aided institutions that are not administered by linguistic or religious minorities. Regulations that can be framed relating to minority institutions will be considered while examining the merit and effect of Article 30 of the Constitution.

Private Unaided Non-Minority Educational Institutions

Private education is one of the most dynamic and fastest growing segments of post-secondary education at the turn of the twenty-first century. A combination of unprecedented demand for access to higher education and the inability or unwillingness of government to provide the necessary support has brought private higher education to the forefront. Private institutions, with a long history in many countries, are expanding in scope and number, and are becoming increasingly important in parts of the world that relied almost entirely on the public sector.

Not only has demand overwhelmed the ability of the governments to provide education, there has also been a significant change in the way that higher education is perceived. The idea of an academic degree as a "private good" that benefits the individual rather than a "public good" for society is now widely accepted. The logic of today's economics and an ideology of privatization have contributed to the resurgence of private higher education, and the establishing of private institutions where none or very few existed before.

The right to establish and administer broadly comprises of the following rights:-

(a) to admit students:

(b) to set up a reasonable fee structure:

(c) to constitute a governing body;

(d) to appoint staff (teaching and non-teaching); and

(e) to take action if there is dereliction of duty on the part of any employees.

A University Education Commission was appointed on 4th November, 1948, having Dr. S. Radhakrishnan as its Chairman and nine other renowned educationists as its members. The terms of reference, inter alia, included matters relating to means and objects of university education and research in India and maintenance of higher standards of teaching and examining in universities and colleges under their control. In the report submitted by this Commission, in paras 29 and 31, it referred to autonomy in education which reads as follows:-

88

"University Autonomy. -- Freedom of individual development is the basis of democracy. Exclusive control of education by the State has been an important factor in facilitating the maintenance of totalitarian tyrannies. In such States institutions of higher learning controlled and managed by governmental agencies act like mercenaries, promote the political purposes of the State, make them acceptable to an increasing number of their populations and supply then with the weapons they need. We must resist, in the interests of our own democracy, the trend towards the governmental domination of the educational process.

Higher educational is, undoubtedly, an obligation of the State but State aid is not to be confused with State control over academic policies and practices. Intellectual progress demands the maintenance of the spirit of free inquiry. The pursuit and practice of truth regardless of consequences has been the ambition of universities. Their prayer is that of the dying Goethe: "More light," or that Ajax in the mist "Light, though I perish in the light.

xxxxx xxx xxx

The respect in which the universities of Great Britain are held is due to the freedom from governmental interference which they enjoy constitutionally and actually. Our universities should be released from the control of politics.

Liberal Education. -- All education is expected to be liberal. It should free us from the shackles of ignorance, prejudice and unfounded belief. If we are incapable of achieving the good life, it is due to faults in our inward being, to the darkness in us. The process of education is the slow conquering of this darkness. To lead us from darkness to light, to free us from every kind of domination except that of reason, is the aim of education."

There cannot be a better exposition than what has been observed by these renowned educationists with regard to autonomy in education. The aforesaid passage clearly shows that the governmental domination of the educational process must be resisted. Another pithy observation of the Commission was that state aid was not to be confused with state control over academic policies and practices. The observations referred to hereinabove clearly contemplate educational institutions soaring to great heights in pursuit of intellectual excellence and being free from unnecessary governmental controls.

With regard to the core components of the rights under Article 19 and 26(a), it must be held that while the state has the right to prescribe qualifications necessary for admission, private unaided colleges have the right to admit students of their choice, subject to an objective and rational procedure of selection and the compliance of conditions, if any, requiring admission of a small percentage of students belonging to weaker sections of the society by granting them feeships or scholarships, if not granted by the Government.

Furthermore, in setting up a reasonable fee structure, the element of profiteering is not as yet accepted in Indian conditions. The fee structure must take into consideration the need to generate funds to be utilized for the betterment and growth of the educational institution, the betterment of education in that institution and to provide facilities necessary for the benefit of the students. In any event, a private institution will have the right to constitute its own governing body, for which qualifications may be prescribed by the state or the concerned university. It will, however, be objectionable if the state retains the power to nominate specific individuals on governing bodies. Nomination by the state, which could be on a political basis, will be an inhibiting factor for private enterprise to embark upon the occupation of establishing and administering educational institutions. For the same reasons, nomination of teachers either directly by the department or through a service commission will be an unreasonable inroad and an unreasonable restrictions on the attorney of the private unaided educational institution.

The right to establish an educational institution can be regulated; but such regulatory measures must, in general, be to ensure the maintenance of proper academic standards, atmosphere and infrastructure (including qualified staff) and the prevention of mal-administration by those in charge of management.

The fixing of a rigid fee structure, dictating the formation and composition of a government body, compulsory nomination of teachers and staff for appointment or nominating students for admissions would be unacceptable restrictions.

The Constitution recognizes the right of the individual or religious denomination, or a religious or linguistic minority to establish an educational institution. If aid or financial assistance is not sought, then such institution will be a private unaided institution. Although, in Unni Krishnan's case, the Court emphasized the important role played by private unaided institutions and the need for private funding, in the scheme that was framed, restrictions were placed on some of the important ingredients relating to the functioning of an educational institution. There can be no doubt that in seeking affiliation or recognition, the Board or the university or the affiliating or recognizing authority can lay down conditions consistent with the requirement to ensure the excellence of education. It can, for instance, indicate the quality of the teachers by prescribing the minimum qualifications that they must possess, and the courses of study and curricula. It can, for the same reasons, also stipulate the existence of infrastructure sufficient for its growth, as a pre-requisite. But the essence of a private educational institution is the autonomy that the institution must have in its management and administration. There, necessarily, has to be a difference in the administration of private unaided institutions and the government-aided institutions. Whereas in the latter case, the Government will have greater say in the administration, including admissions and fixing of fees, in the case of private unaided institutions, maximum autonomy in the day-to-day administration has to be with the private unaided institutions. Bureaucratic or governmental interference in the administration of such an institution will undermine its independence. While an educational institution is not a business, in order to examine the degree of independence that can be given to a recognized educational institution, like any private entity that does not seek aid or assistance from the Government, and that exists by virtue of the funds generated by it, including its loans or borrowings, it is important to note that the essential ingredients of the management of the private institution include the recruiting students and staff, and the quantum of fee that is to be charged.

An educational institution is established for the purpose of imparting education of the type made available by the institution. Different courses of study are usually taught by teachers who have to be recruited as per qualifications that may be prescribed. It is no secret that better working conditions will attract better teachers. More amenities will ensure that better students seek admission to that institution. One cannot lose sight of the fact that providing good amenities to the students in the form of competent teaching faculty and other infrastructure costs money. It has, therefore, to be left to the institution, if it chooses not to seek any aid from the government, to determine the scale of fee that it can charge from the students. One also cannot lose sight of the fact that we live in a competitive world today, where professional education is in demand. A large number of professional and other institutions have been started by private parties who do not seek any governmental aid. In a sense a prospective students has various options open to him/her where, therefore, normally economic forces have a role to play. The decision on the fee to be charged must necessarily be left to the private educational institution that does not seek or is not dependent upon any funds from the government.

Inasmuch as the occupation of education is, in a sense, regarded as charitable, the government can provide regulations that will ensure excellence in education, while forbidding the charging of capitation fee and profiteering by the institution. Since the object of setting up an educational institution is by definition "charitable", it is clear that an educational institution cannot charge such a fee as is not required for the purpose of fulfilling that object. To put it differently, in the establishment of an educational institution, the object should not be to make a profit, inasmuch as education is essentially charitable in nature. There can, however, be a reasonable revenue surplus, which may be generated by the educational institution for the purpose of development of education and expansion of the institution.

For admission into any professional institution, merit must play an important role. While it may not be normally possible to judge the merit of the applicant who seeks admission into a school, while seeking admission to a professional institution and to become a competent professional, it is necessary that meritorious candidates are not unfairly treated or put at a disadvantage by preferences shown to less meritorious but more influential applicants. Excellence in professional education would require that greater emphasis be laid on the merit of a student seeking admission. Appropriate regulations for this purpose may be made keeping in view the other observations made in this judgment in the context of admissions to unaided institutions.

Merit is usually determined, for admission to professional and higher education colleges, by either the marks that the student obtains at the qualifying examination or school leaving certificate stage followed by the interview, or by a common entrance test conducted by the institution, or in the case of professional colleges, by government agencies.

Education is taught at different levels from primary to professional. It is, therefore, obvious that government regulations for all levels or types of educational institutions cannot be identical; so also, the extent of control or regulation could be greater vis-a-vis[152] aided institutions.

In the case of unaided private schools, maximum autonomy has to be with the management with regard to administration, including the right of appointment, disciplinary powers, admission of students and the fees to be charged.

---

152 **Meaning of vis-a-vis:**
    Face to face with; opposite to.

At the school level, it is not possible to grant admission on the basis of merit. It is no secret that the examination results at all levels of unaided private schools, notwithstanding the stringent regulations of the governmental authorities, are far superior to the results of the government-maintained schools. There is no compulsion on students to attend private schools. The rush for admission is occasioned by the standards maintained in such schools, and recognition of the fact that state-run schools do not provide the same standards of education. The State says that it has no funds to establish institutions at the same level of excellence as private schools. But by curtaining the income of such private schools, it disables those schools from affording the best facilities because of a lack of funds. If this lowering of standards from excellence to a level of mediocrity is to be avoided, the state has to provide the difference which, brings back the vicious circle to the original problem, viz., the lack of state funds. The solution would appear to lie in the States not using their scanty resources to prop up institutions that are able to otherwise maintain themselves out of the fees charged, but in improving the facilities and infrastructure of state-run schools and in subsidizing the fees payable by the students there. It is in the interest of the general public that more good quality schools are established; autonomy and non-regulation of the school administration in the right of appointment, admission of the students and the fee to be charged will ensure that more such institutions are established. The fear that if a private school is allowed to charge fees commensurate with the fees affordable, the degrees would be "purchasable" is an unfounded one since the standards of education can be and are controllable through the regulations relating to recognition, affiliation and common final examinations.

There is a need for private enterprise in non-professional college education as well. At present, insufficient number of undergraduate colleges are being and have been established, one of the inhibiting factors being that there is a lack of autonomy due to government regulations. It will not be wrong to presume that the numbers of professional colleges are growing at a faster rate than the number of undergraduate and non-professional colleges. While it is desirable that there should be a sufficient number of professional colleges, it should also be possible for private unaided undergraduate colleges that are non-technical in nature to have maximum autonomy similar to a school.

An educational institution is established only for the purpose of imparting education to the students. In such an institution, it is necessary for all to maintain discipline and abide by the rules and regulations that have been lawfully framed. The teachers are like foster-parents who are required to look after, cultivate and guide the students in their pursuit of education. The teachers and the institution exist for the students and not vice versa. Once this principle is kept in mind, it must follow that it becomes imperative for the teaching and other staff of an educational institution to perform their duties properly, and for the benefit of the students. Where allegations of misconduct are made, it is imperative that a disciplinary enquiry is conducted, and that a decision is taken. In the case of a private institution, the relationship between the Management and the employees is contractual in nature. A teacher, if the contract so provides, can be proceeded against, and appropriate disciplinary action can be taken if the misconduct of the teacher is proved. Considering the nature of the duties and keeping the principle of natural justice in mind for the purposes of establishing misconduct and taking action thereon, it is imperative that a fair domestic enquiry is conducted. It is only on the basis of the result of the disciplinary enquiry that the management will be entitled to take appropriate action. We see no reason why the Management of a private unaided educational should seek the consent or approval of any governmental authority before taking any such action. In the ordinary relationship of master and servant, governed by the terms of a contract of employment, anyone who is guilty of breach of the terms can be proceeded against and appropriately relief can be sought. Normally, the aggrieved party would approach a court of law and seek redress. In the case of educational institutions, however, requiring a teacher or a member of the staff to go to a civil court for the purpose of seeking redress is not in the interest of general education. Disputes between the management and the staff of educational institutions must be decided speedily, and without the excessive incurring of costs. It would, therefore, be appropriate that an educational Tribunal be set up in each district in a State, to enable the aggrieved teacher to file an appeal, unless there already exists such an educational tribunal in a State -- the object being that the teacher should not suffer through the substantial costs that arise because of the location of the tribunal; if the tribunals are limited in number, they can hold circuit/camp sittings in different districts to achieve this objective. Till a specialized tribunal is set up, the right of filing the appeal would lie before the District Judge or Additional District Judge as notified by the government. It will not be necessary for the institution to get prior permission or ex post facto approval of a governmental authority while taking disciplinary action against a teacher or any other employee. The State Government shall determine, in consultation with the High Court, the judicial forum in which an aggrieved teacher can file an appeal against the decision of the management concerning disciplinary action or termination of service.

The reputation of an educational institution is established by the qualify of its faculty and students, and the educational and other facilities that the colleges has to offer. The private educational institutions have a personality of their own, and in order to maintain their atmosphere and traditions, it is but necessary that they must have the right to choose and select the students who can be admitted to their courses of studies. It is for this reason that in the St. Stephen's College[153] case, Supreme Court upheld the scheme whereby a cut-off percentage was fixed for admission, after which the students were interviewed and thereafter selected. While an educational institution cannot grant admission on its whims and fancies, and must follow some identifiable or reasonable methodology of admitting the students, any scheme, rule or regulation that does not give the institution the right to reject candidates who might otherwise be qualified according to say their performance in an entrance test, would be an unreasonable restriction under Article 19(6), though appropriate guidelines/modalities can be prescribed for holding the entrance test a fair manner. Even when students are required to be selected on the basis of merit, the ultimate decision to grant admission to the students who have otherwise qualified for the grant of admission must be left with the educational institution concerned. However, when the institution rejects such students, such rejection must not be whimsical or for extraneous reasons.

In the case of private unaided educational institution, the authority granting recognition or affiliation can certainly lay down conditions for the grant of recognition or affiliation; these conditions must pertain broadly to academic and educational matters and welfare of students and teachers - but how the private unaided institutions are to run is a matter of administration to be taken care of by the Management of those institutions.

Private Unaided Professional Colleges

It would be unfair to apply the same rules and regulations regulating admission to both aided and unaided professional institutions. It must be borne in mind that unaided professional institutions are entitled to autonomy in their administration while, at the same time, they do not forgo or discard the principle of merit. It would, therefore, be permissible for the university or the government, at the time of granting recognition, to require a private unaided institution to provide for merit-based selection while, at

---

153 St. Stephen's College v. University of Delhi, MANU/SC/0319/1992

the same time, giving the Management sufficient discretion in admitting students. This can be done through various methods. For instance, a certain percentage of the seats can be reserved for admission by the Management out of those students who have passed the common entrance test held by itself or by the State/University and have applied to the college concerned for admission, while the rest of the seats may be filled up on the basis of counselling by the state agency. This will incidentally take care of poorer and backward sections of the society. The prescription of percentage for this purpose has to be done by the government according to the local needs and different percentage can be fixed for minority unaided and non-minority unaided and professional colleges. The same principles may be applied to other non-professional but unaided educational institutions viz., graduation and post-graduation non-professional colleges or institutes.

In such professional unaided institutions, the Management will have the right to select teachers as per the qualifications and eligibility conditions laid down by the State/University subject to adoption of a rational procedure of selection. A rational fee structure should be adopted by the Management, which would not be entitled to charge a capitation fee. Appropriate machinery can be devised by the state or university to ensure that no capitation fee is charged and that there is no profiteering, though a reasonable surplus for the furtherance of education is permissible. Conditions granting recognition or affiliation can broadly cover academic and educational matters including the welfare of students and teachers.

It is well established all over the world that those who seek professional education must pay for it. The number of seats available in government and government-aided colleges is very small, compared to the number of persons seeking admission to the medical and engineering colleges. All those eligible and deserving candidates who could not be accommodated in government colleges would stand deprived of professional education. This void in the field of medical and technical education has been filled by institutions that are established in different places with the aid of donations and the active part taken by public-minded individuals. The object of establishing an institution has thus been to provide technical or professional education to the deserving candidates, and is not necessarily a commercial venture. In order that this intention is meaningful, the institution must be recognized. At the school level, the recognition or affiliation has to be sought from the educational authority or the body that conducts the school-leaving examination. It is only on the basis of that examination that a school-leaving certificate is granted, which enables a student to seek admission in further courses of study after school. A college or a professional educational institution has to get recognition from the concerned university, which normally requires certain conditions to be fulfilled before recognition. It has been held that conditions of affiliation or recognition, which pertain to the academic and educational character of the institution and ensure uniformity, efficiency and excellence in educational courses are valid, and that they do not violate even the provisions of Article 30 of the Constitution; but conditions that are laid down for granting recognition should not be such as may lead to governmental control of the administration of the private educational institutions.

Private Aided Professional Institutions (non-minority)

While giving aid to professional institutions, it would be permissible for the authority giving aid to prescribe by rules or regulations, the conditions on the basis of which admission will be granted to different aided colleges by virtue of merit, coupled with the reservation policy of the state. The merit may be determined either through a common entrance test conducted by the University or the Government followed by counseling, or on the basis of an entrance test conducted by individual institutions - the method to be followed is for the university or the government to decide. The authority may also device other means to ensure that admission is granted to an aided professional institution on the basis of merit. In the case of such institutions, it will be permissible for the government or the university to provide that consideration should be shown to the weaker sections of the society.

Once aid is granted to a private professional educational institution, the government or the state agency, as a condition of the grant of aid, can put fetters on the freedom in the matter of administration and management of the institution. The state, which gives aid to an educational institution, can impose such conditions as are necessary for the proper maintenance of the high standards of education as the financial burden is shared by the state. The state would also be under an obligation to protect the interest of the teaching and non-teaching staff. In many states, there are various statutory provisions to regulate the functioning of such educational institutions where the States give, as a grant or aid, a substantial proportion of the revenue expenditure including salary, pay and allowances of teaching and non-teaching staff. It would be its responsibility to ensure that the teachers working in those institutions are governed by proper service conditions. The state, in the case of such aided institutions, has ample power to regulate the method of selection and appointment of teachers after prescribing requisite qualifications for the same. Ever since In Re The Kerala Education Bill, 1957, [1959]1SCR995 Court has upheld, in the case of aided institutions, those regulations that served the interests of students and teachers. Checks on the administration may be necessary in order to ensure that the administration is efficient and sound and will serve the academic needs of the institutions. In other words, rules and regulations that promote good administration and prevent mal-administration can be formulated so as to promote the efficiency of teachers, discipline and fairness in administration and to preserve harmony among affiliated institutions. At the same time it has to be ensured that even an aided institution does not become a government-owned and controlled institution. Normally, the aid that is granted is relatable to the pay and allowances of the teaching staff. In addition, the Management of the private aided institutions has to incur revenue and capital expenses. Such aided institutions cannot obtain that extent of autonomy in relation to management and administration as would be available to a private unaided institution, but at the same time, it cannot also be treated as an educational institution departmentally run by government or as a wholly owned and controlled government institution and interfere with Constitution of the governing bodies or thrusting the staff without reference to Management.

Other Aided Institutions

There are a large number of educational institutions, like schools and non-professional colleges, which cannot operate without the support of aid from the state. Although these institutions may have been established by philanthropists or other public-spirited persons, it becomes necessary, in order to provide inexpensive education to the students, to seek aid from the state. In such cases, as those of the professional aided institutions referred to hereinabove, the Government would be entitled to make regulations relating to the terms and conditions of employment of the teaching and non-teaching staff whenever the aid for the posts is given by the State as well as admission procedures. Such rules and regulations can also provide for the reasons and the manner in which a teacher or any other member of the staff can be removed. in other words, the autonomy of a private aided institution would be less than that of an unaided institution.

In order to determine the existence of a religious or linguistic minority in relation to article 30, what is to be the unit - the state or the country as a whole?

Article 30(1) deals with religious minorities and linguistic minorities. The opening words of Article 30(1) make it clear that religious and linguistic minorities have been put at par, insofar as that Article is concerned. Therefore, whatever the unit - whether a state or the whole of India - for determining a linguistic minority, it would be the same in relation to a religious minority. India is divided into different linguistic states. The states have been carved out on the basis of the language of the majority of persons of that region. For example, Andhra Pradesh was established on the basis of the language of that region. viz., Telugu. "Linguistic minority" can, therefore, logically only be in relation to a particular State. If the determination of "linguistic minority" for the purpose of Article 30 is to be in relation to the whole of India, then within the State of Andhra Pradesh, Telugu speakers will have to be regarded as a "linguistic minority". This will clearly be contrary to the concept of linguistic states.

If, therefore, the state has to be regarded as the unit for determining "linguistic minority" vis-a-vis Article 30, then with "religious minority" being on the same footing, it is the state in relation to which the majority or minority status will have to be determined.

In the Kerala Education Bill case, the question as to whether the minority community was to be determined on the basis of the entire population of India, or on the basis of the population of the State forming a part of the Union was posed at page 1047. It had been contended by the State of Kerala that for claiming the status of minority, the persons must numerically be a minority in the particular region in which the education institution was situated, and that the locality or ward or town where the institution was to be situated had to be taken as the unit to determine the minority community. No final opinion on this question was expressed, but it was observed at page 1050 that as the Kerala Education Bill "extends to the whole of the State of Kerala and consequently the minority must be determined by reference to the entire population of that State."

The Forty-Second Amendment to the Constitution included education in the Concurrent List under Entry 25. Would this in any way change the position with regard to the determination of a "religious" or "linguistic minority" for the purposes of Article 30.

As a result of the insertion of Entry 25 into List III, Parliament can now legislate in relation to education, which was only a state subject previously. The jurisdiction of the Parliament is to make laws for the whole or a part of India. It is well recognized that geographical classification is not violative of Article 14. It would, therefore, be possible that, with respect to a particular State or group of States, Parliament may legislate in relation to education. However, Article 30 gives the right to a linguistic or religious minority of a State to establish and administer educational institutions of their choice. The minority for the purpose of Article 30 cannot have different meanings depending upon who is legislating. Language being the basis for the establishment of different states for the purposes of Article 30 a "linguistic minority" will have to be determined in relation to the state in which the educational institution is sought to be established. The position with regard to the religious minority is similar, since both religious and linguistic minorities have been put at par in Article 30.

To what extent can the rights of aided private minority institutions to administer be regulated?

Article 25[154] gives all persons the freedom of conscience and the right to freely profess, practice and propagate religion. This right, however, is not absolute. The opening words of Article 25(1) make this right subject to public order, morality and health, and also to the other provisions of Part III of the Constitution. This would mean that the right given to a person under 25(1) can be curtailed or regulated if the exercise of that right would violate other provisions of Part III of the Constitution, or if the exercise thereof is to in consonance with public order, morality and health. The general law made by the government contains provisions relating to public order, morality and health; these would have to be complied with, and cannot be violated by any person in exercise of his freedom of conscience or his freedom to profess, practice and propagate religion. For example, a person cannot propagate his religion in such a manner as to denigrate another religion or bring about dissatisfaction amongst people.

---

154 **Article 25 in The Constitution Of India 1949**
   25. Freedom of conscience and free profession, practice and propagation of religion
   (1) Subject to public order, morality and health and to the other provisions of this Part, all persons are equally entitled to freedom of conscience and the right freely to profess, practise and propagate religion
   (2) Nothing in this article shall affect the operation of any existing law or prevent the State from making any law
   (a) regulating or restricting any economic, financial, political or other secular activity which may be associated with religious practice;
   (b) providing for social welfare and reform or the throwing open of Hindu religious institutions of a public character to all classes and sections of Hindus Explanation I The wearing and carrying of kirpans shall be deemed to be included in the profession of the Sikh religion Explanation II In sub clause (b) of clause reference to Hindus shall be construed as including a reference to persons professing the Sikh, Jaina or Buddhist religion, and the reference to Hindu religious institutions shall be construed accordingly

Article 25(2) gives specific power to the state to make any law regulating or restricting any economic, financial, political or other secular activity, which may be associated with religious practice as provided by Sub-clause (a) of Article 25(2). This is a further curtailment of the right to profess, practice and propagate religion conferred on the persons under Article 25(1). Article 25(2)(a) covers only a limited area associated with religious practice, in respect of which a law can be made. A careful reading of Article 25(2)(a) indicates that it does not prevent the State from making any law in relation to the religious practice as such. The limited jurisdiction granted by Article 25(2) relates to the making of a law in relation to economic, financial, political or other secular activities associated with the religious practice.

The freedom to manage religious affairs is provided by Article 26. This Article gives the right to every religious denomination, or any section thereof, to exercise the rights that it stipulates. However, this right has to be exercised in a manner that is in conformity with public order, morality and health. Clause (a) of Article 26 gives a religious denomination the right to establish and maintain institutions for religious and charitable purposes. There is no dispute that the establishment of an educational institution comes within the meaning of the expression "charitable purpose". therefore, while Article 25(1) grants the freedom of conscience and the right to profess, practice and propagate religion, Article 26 can be said to be complementary to it, and provides for every religious denomination, or any section thereof, to exercise the rights mentioned therein. This is because Article 26 does not deal with the right of an individual, but is confined to a religious denomination. Article 26 refers to a denomination of any religion, whether it is a majority or a minority religion, just as Article 25 refers to all persons, whether they belong to the majority or a minority religion. Article 26 gives the right to majority religious denominations, as well as to minority religious denominations, to exercise the rights contained therein.

Secularism[155] being one of the important basic features of our Constitution, Article 27 provides that no person shall be compelled to pay any taxes, the proceeds of which are specifically appropriated for the payment of expenses for the promotion and maintenance of any particular religion or religious denomination. The manner in which the Article has been framed does not prohibit the state from enacting a law to incur expenses for the promotion or maintenance of any particular religion or religious denomination, but

---

155 The view that religious considerations should be excluded from civil affairs or public education.

specifies that by that law, no person can be compelled to pay any tax, the proceeds of which are to be so utilized. In other words, if there is a tax for the promotion or maintenance of any particular religion or religious denomination, no person an be compelled to pay any such tax.

Article 28(1) prohibits any educational institution, which is wholly maintained out of state funds, to provide for religious instruction. Moral education dissociation from any demon national doctrine is not prohibited; but, as the state is intended to be secular, an educational institution wholly maintained out of state funds cannot impart or provide for any religious instruction.

The exception to Article 28(1) is contained in Article 28(2). Article 28(2) deals with cases where, by an endowment or trust, an institution is established, and the terms of the endowment or the trust require the imparting of religious instruction, and where that institution is administered by the state. In such a case, the prohibition contained in Article 28(1) does not apply. If the administration of such an institution is voluntarily given to the government, or the government, for a good reason and in accordance with law, assumes or takes over the management of that institution, say on account of mal-administration, then the government, on assuming the administration of the institution, would be obliged to continue with the imparting of religious instruction as provided by the endowment or the trust.

While Article 28(1) and Article 28(2) relate to institutions that are wholly maintained out of state funds, Article 28(3) deals with an educational institution that is recognized by the state or receives aid out of state funds. Article 28(3) gives the person attending any educational institution the right not to take part in any religious instruction, which may be imparted by an institution recognized by the state, or receiving aid from the state. Such a person also has the right not to attend any religious worship that may be conducted in such an institution, or in any premises attached thereto, unless such a person, or if he/she is a minor, his/her guardian, has given his/her consent. The reading of Article 28(3) clearly shows that no person attending an educational institution can be required to take part in any religious instruction or any religious worship, unless the person or his/her guardian has given his/her consent thereto, in a case where the educational institution has been recognized by the state or receives aid out of its funds. We have seen that Article 26(a) gives the religious denomination the right to establish an educational institution, the religious denomination being either of the majority community or minority community. In any institution, whether established by the majority or a minority religion, if religious instruction in imparted, no student can be compelled to take part in the said religious instruction or in any religious worship. An individual has the absolute right not to be compelled to take part in any religious instruction or worship. Article 28(3) thereby recognizes the right of an individual to practice or profess his own religion. In other words, in matters relating to religious instruction or worship, there can be no compulsion where the educational institution is either recognized by the state or receives aid from the state.

Articles 29 and 30 are a group of articles relating to cultural and educational rights. Article 29(1) gives the right to any section of the citizens residing in India or any part thereof, and having a distinct language, script or culture of its own, to conserve the same. Article 29(1) does not refer to any religion, even though the marginal note of the Article mentions the interests of minorities. Article 29(1) essentially refers to sections of citizens who have a distinct language script or culture, even though their religion may not be the same. The common thread that runs through Article 29(1) in language, script or culture, and not religion. For example, if in any part of the country, there is a section of society that has a distinct language, they are entitled to conserve the same, even though the persons having that language may profess different religions. Article 29(1) gives the right to all sections of citizens, whether they are in a minority or the majority religions, to conserve their language, script or culture.

In the exercise of this right to converse the language, script or culture, that section of the society can set up educational institutions. The right to establish and maintain institutions of its choice is a necessary concomitant to the right conferred by Article 30. The right under Article 30 is not absolute. Article 29(2) provides that, where any educational institution is maintained by the state or receives aid out of state funds no citizen shall be denied admission on the grounds only of religion, race, caste, language or any of them. The use of the expression "any educational institution" in Article 29(2) would refer to any educational institution established by anyone, but which is maintained by the state or receives aid out of state funds. In other words, on a plain reading, state-maintained or aided educational institutions, whether established by the Government or the majority or a minority community cannot deny admission to a citizen on the grounds only of religion, race, caste or language.

The right of the minorities to establish and administer educational institutions is provided for by Article 30(1). To some extent, Article 26(1)

(a) and Article 30(1) overlap, insofar as they relate to the establishment of educational institutions but whereas Article 26 gives the right both to the majority as well as minority communities to establish and maintain institutions for charitable purposes, which would inter alia, include educational institutions, Article 30(1) refers to the right of minorities to establish and maintain educational institutions of their choice. Another difference between Article 26 and Article 30 is that whereas Article 26 refers only to religious denominations, Article 30 contains the right of religious as well as linguistic minorities to establish and administer educational institutions of their choice.

Article 30(1) bestows on the minorities, whether based on religion or language, the right to establish and administer educational institution of their choice. Unlike Article 25 and 26, Article 30(1) does not specifically state that the right under Article 30(1) is subject to public order, morality and health or to other provisions of Part III. This Sub-Article also does not specifically mention that the right to establish and administer a minority educational institution would be subject to any rules or regulations.

Can Article 30(1) be so read as to mean that it contains an absolute right of the minorities, whether based on religion or language, to establish and administer educational institutions in any manner they desire, and without being obliged to comply with the provisions of any law? Des Article 30(1) give the religious or linguistic minorities a right to establish an educational institution that propagates religious or racial bigotry or ill will amongst the people? Can the right under Article 30(1) be so exercised that it is opposed to public morality or health? In the exercise of its right, would the minority while establishing educational institutions not be bound by town planning rules and regulations? Can they construct and maintain buildings in any manner they desire without complying with the provisions of the building by-laws or health regulations?

In order to interpret Article 30 and its interplay, it any, with Article 29, our attention was drawn to the Constituent Assembly Debates. While referring to them, the learned Solicitor General submitted that the provisions of Article 29(2) were intended to be applicable to minority institutions seeking protection of Article 30. He argued that if any educational institution sought aid, it could not deny admission only on the ground of religion, race, caste or language and, consequently giving a preference to the minority over more meritorious non-minority students was impermissible. It is now necessary to refer to some of the decisions of this Court insofar as they interpret Articles 29 and 30, and to examine whether any creases therein need ironing out.

In The State of Madras v. Srimathi Champakam Dorairajan, [1951]2SCR525 the State had issued an order, which provided that admission to students to engineering and medical colleges in the State should be decided by the Selection Committee strictly on the basis of the number of seats fixed for different communities. While considering the validity of this order Court interpreted Article 29(2) and held that if admission was refused only on the grounds of religion, race, caste, language or any of them, then there was a clear breach of the fundamental right under Article 29(2). The said order was construed as being violative of Article 29(2), because students who did not fall in the particular categories were to be denied admission. In this connection it was observed as follows:-

".....So far as those seats are concerned, the petitioners are denied admission into any of them, not on any ground other than the sole ground of their being Brahmins and not being members of the community for whom those reservations were made....."

This government order was held to be violative of the Constitution and constitutive of a clear breach of Article 29(2). Article 30 did not come up for consideration in that case.

In The State of Bombay v. Bombay Education Society and Ors., [1955]1SCR568, the State had issued a circular, the operative portion of which directed that no primary or secondary school could, from the date of that circular admit to a class where English was used as a medium of instruction, any pupil other than pupils belonging to a section of citizens, the language of whom was English, viz, Anglo-Indians and citizens of non-Asiatic descent. The validity of the circular was challenged while admission was refused, inter alia, to a member of the Gujarati Hindu Community. A number of writ petitions were filed and the High Court allowed them. In an application filed by the State of Bombay, this Court had to consider whether the said circular was ultra vires Article 29(2). In deciding this question, the Court analyzed the provisions of Articles 29(2) and 30, and repelled the contention that Article 29(2) guaranteed the right only to the citizens of the minority group. It was observed, in this connection, at page 579, as follows:

"..... The language of Article 29(2) is wide and unqualified and may well cover all citizens whether they belong to the majority or minority group. Article 15 protects all citizens against the State whereas the protection of Article 29(2)

extends against the State or anybody who denies the right conferred by it. Further Article 15 protects all citizens against discrimination generally but Article 29(2) is a protection against a particular species of wrong namely denial of admission into educational institutions of the specified kind. In the next place Article 15 is quite general and wide in its terms and applies to all citizens, whether they belong to the majority or minority groups, and gives protection to all the citizens against discrimination by the State on certain specific grounds. Article 29(2) confers a special right on citizens for admission into educational institutions maintained or aided by the State. To limit this right only to citizens belonging to minority groups will be to provide a double protection for such citizens and to hold that the citizens of the majority group have no special educational rights in the nature of a right to be admitted into an educational institution for the maintenance of which they make contributions by way of taxes. We see no cogent reason for such discrimination. The heading under which Articles 29 and 30 are grouped together - namely "Cultural and Educational Rights" is quite general and does not in terms contemplate such differentiation. If the fact that the institution is maintained or aided out of State funds is the basis of this guaranteed right then all citizens, irrespective of whether they belong to the majority or minority groups; are alike entitled to the protection of this fundamental right....."

It is clear from the aforesaid discussion that Court came to the conclusion that in the case of minority educational institutions to which protection was available under Article 30, the provisions of Article 29(2) were indeed applicable. But, it may be seen that the question in the present from i.e., whether in the matter of admissions into aided minority educational institutions, minority students could be preferred to a reasonable extent, keeping in view the special protection given under Article 30(1), did not arise for consideration in that case.

The interplay of Article 29 and Article 30 came up for consideration again before Court in the D.A.V. College case, 1971 (Supp.) SCR 688. Some of the provisions of the Guru Nanak University Act established after the reorganization of the State of Punjab in 1969 provided for the manner in which the governing body was to be constituted; the body was to include a representative of the University and a member of the College. These and some other provisions were challenged on the ground that they were violative of Article 30. In this connection at page 695, it was observed as follows:-

"*It will be observed that Article 29(1) is wider than Article 30(1), in that, while any Section of the citizens including the minorities, can invoke the rights guaranteed under Article 29(1), the rights guaranteed under Article 30(1) are only available to the minorities based on religion or language. It is not necessary for Article 30(1) that the minority should be both a religion minority as well as a linguistic minority. It is sufficient if it is one or the other or both. A reading of these two Articles together would lead us to conclude that a religious or linguistic minority has a right to establish and administer educational institutions of its choice for effectively conserving its distinctive language, script or culture, which right however is subject to the regulatory power of the State for maintaining and facilitating the excellence of its standards. This right is further subject to Clause (2) of Article 29 which provides that no citizen shall be denied admission into any educational institution which is maintained by the State or receives aid out of State funds, on grounds only of religion, race, caste, language or any of them. While this is so these two articles are not inter-linked nor does it permit of their being always read together."*

Though it was observed that Article 30(1) is subject to 29(2), the question whether the preference to minority students is altogether excluded, was not considered.

Whether Article 30 gives a right to ask for a grant or aid from the state, and secondly, if it does get aid, to examine to what extent its autonomy in administration, specifically in the matter of admission to the educational institution established by the community, can be curtailed or regulated.

The grant of aid is not a constitutional imperative. Article 337 only gives the right to assistance by way of grant to the Anglo-Indian community for a specified period of time. If no aid is granted to anyone, Article 30(1) would not justify a demand for aid, and it cannot be said that the absence of aid makes the right under Article 30(1). The founding fathers have not incorporated the right to grants in Article 30, whereas they have done so under Article 337; what, then, is the meaning, scope and effect of Article 30(2)? Article 30(2) only means what it states, viz that a minority institution shall not be discriminated against when aid to educational institutions is granted. In other words the state cannot, when it chooses to grant aid to educational institutions, deny aid to a religious or linguistic minority institution only on the ground that the management of that institution is with the minority. We would, however, like to clarify that if an object surrender of the right to management is made a condition of aid, the denial of aid would be violative of Article 30(2). However, conditions of aid that do not involve a surrender of the substantial right of management would not be inconsistent with constitutional guarantees, even if they indirectly impinge upon some fact of administration. If, however, aid were denied on the ground that the educational institution is under the management of a minority, then such a denial would be completely invalid.

The implication of Article 30(2) is also that it recognizes that the minority nature of the institution should continue, notwithstanding the grant of aid. In other words, when a grant is given to all institutions for imparting secular education, a minority institution is also entitled to receive it subject to the fulfillment of the requisite criteria, and the state gives the grant knowing that a linguistic or minority educational institution will also receive the same. Of course, the state cannot be compelled to grant aid, but the receipt of aid cannot be a reason for altering the nature of character of the incipient educational institution.

This means that the right under Article 30(1) implies that any grant that is given by the state to the minority institution cannot have such conditions attached to it, which will in any way dilute or abridge the rights of the minority institution to establish and administer that institution. The conditions that can normally be permitted to be imposed, on the educational institutions receiving the grant, must be related to the proper utilization of the grant and fulfillment of the objectives of the grant. Any such secular conditions so laid, such as a proper audit with regard to the utilization of the funds and the manner in which the funds are to be utilized, will be applicable and would not dilute the minority status of the educational institutions. Such conditions would be valid if they are also imposed on other educational institutions receiving the grant.

It cannot be argued that no conditions can be imposed while giving aid to a minority institution. Whether it is an institution run by the majority or the minority, all conditions that have relevance to the proper utilization of the grant-in-aid by an educational institution can be imposed. All that Article 30(2) states is that on the ground that an institution is under the management of a minority, whether based on religion or language, grant of aid to that educational institution cannot be discriminated against, if other educational institutions are entitled to received aid. The conditions for grant or non-grant of aid to educational institutions have to be uniformly applied, whether it is a majority-run institution or a minority-run institution.

As in the case of a majority-run institution, the moment a minority institution obtains a grant of aid, Article 28 of the Constitution comes into play. When an educational institution is maintained out of State funds, no religious institution can be provided therein. Article 28(1) does not state that it applies only to educational institutions that are not established or maintained by religious or linguistic minorities. Furthermore, upon the receipt of aid, the provisions of Article 28(3) would apply to all educational institutions whether run by the minorities or the non-minorities. Article 28(3) is the right of a person studying in a state recognized institution or in an educational institution receiving aid from state funds, not to take part in any religious instruction, if imparted by such institution, without his/her consent (or his/her guardian's consent if such a person is a minor). Just as Article 28(1) and (3) become applicable the moment any educational institution takes aid, likewise, Article 29(2) would also be attracted and become applicable to an educational institution maintained by the state or receiving aid out of state funds. It was strenuously contended that the right to give admission is one of the essential ingredients of the right to administer conferred on the religious or linguistic minority, and that this right should not be curtailed in any manner. It is difficult to accept this contention. If Article 23(1) and (3) apply to a minority institution that receives aid out of state funds, there is nothing in the language of Article 30 that would make the provisions of Article 29(2) inapplicable. Like Article 28(1) and Article 28(3), Article 29(2) refers to "any educational institution maintained by the State or receiving aid out of State funds". A minority institution would fall within the ambit of Article 29(2) in the same manner in which Article 28(1) and Article 28(3) would be applicable to an aided minority institution. it is true that one of the rights to administer an educational institution is to grant admission to the students. As long as an educational institution, whether belonging to the minority or the majority community, does not receive aid, it would, in our opinion, be its right and discretion to grant admission to such students as it chooses or selects subject to what has been clarified before. Out of the various rights that the minority institution has in the administration of the institution, Article 29(2) curtails the right to grant admission to a certain extent. By virtue of Article 29(2), no citizen can be denied admission by an aided minority institution on the grounds only of religion, race, caste, language or any of them. It is no doubt true that Article 29(2) does curtail one of the powers of the minority institution, but on receiving aid, some of the rights that an unaided minority institution has are also curtailed by Article 28(1) and 28(3). A minority educational institution has a right to impart religious instruction - this right is taken away by Article 28(1), if that minority institution is maintained wholly out of state funds. Similarly on receiving aid out of state funds or on being recognized by the state, the absolute right of a minority institution requiring a student to attend religious instruction is curtailed by Article 28(3). If the curtailment of the right to administer a minority institution on receiving aid or being wholly maintained out of state funds as provided by Article 28 is valid, there is no reason why Article 29(2) should not be held to be applicable. There is nothing in the language of Article 28(1) and (3), Article 29(2) and Article 30 to suggest that on receiving aid, Article 28(1) and (3) will apply, but Article 29(2) will not. therefore, the contention that the institutions covered by Article 30 are outside the injunction of Article 29(2) cannot be accepted.

What is the true scope and effect of Article 29(2)? Article 29(2) is capable of two interpretations--one interpretation, which is put forth by the Solicitor General and the other counsel for the different States, is that a minority institution receiving aid cannot deny admission to any citizen on the grounds of religion, race, caste, language or any of them. In other words, the minority institution, once it takes any aid, cannot make any reservation for its own community or show a preference at the time of admission, i.e., if the educational institution was a private unaided minority institution, it is free to admit all students of its own community, but once aid is received, Article 29(2) makes it obligatory on the institution not to deny admission to a citizen just because he does not belong to the minority community that has established the institution.

The other interpretation that is put forth is that Article 29(2) is a protection against discrimination on the ground of religion, race, caste or language, and does not in any way come into play where the minority institution prefers students of its choice. To put it differently, denying admission, even though seats are available, on the ground of the applicant's religion, race, caste or language, is prohibited, but preferring students of minority groups does not violate Article 29(2).

Both Articles 29 and 30 from a part of the fundamental rights Chapter in Part III of the Constitution. Article 30 is confined to minorities, be it religious or linguistic, and unlike Article 29(1), the right available under the said Article cannot be availed by any section of citizens. The main distinction between Article 29(1) and Article 30(1) is that in the former, the right is confined to conservation of language, script or culture. As was observed in the Father W. Proost case, the right given by Article 29(1) is fortified by Article 30(1), insofar as minorities are concerned. In the St. Xaviers College case, it was held that the right to establish an educational institution is not confined to conservation of language, script or culture.

When constitutional provisions are interpreted, it has to be borne in mind that the interpretation should be such as to further the object of their incorporation. They cannot be read in isolation and have to be read harmoniously to provide meaning and purpose. They cannot be interpreted in a manner that renders another provision redundant. If necessary, a purposive and harmonious interpretation should be given.

Although the right to administer includes within it a right to grant admission to students of their choice under Article 30(1), when such a minority institution is granted the facility of receiving grant-in-aid, Article 29(2) would apply, and necessarily, therefore, one of the right of administration of the minorities would be eroded to some extent. Article 30(2) is an injunction against the state not to discriminate against the minority educational institution and prevent it from receiving aid on the ground that the institution is under the management of a minority. While, therefore, a minority educational institution receiving grant-in-aid would not be completely outside the discipline of Article 29(2) of the Constitution by no stretch of imagination can the rights guaranteed under Article 30(1) be annihilated. It is this context that some interplay between Article 29(2) and Article 30(1) is required. As observed quite aptly in St. Stephen's case "the fact that Article 29(2) applies to minorities as well as non-minorities does not mean that it was intended to nullify the special right guaranteed to minorities in Article 30(1)." The word "only" used in Article 29(2) is of considerable significance and has been used for some avowed purpose. Denying admission to non-minorities for the purpose of accommodating minority students to a reasonable extent will not be only on grounds of religion etc., but is primarily meant to preserve the minority character of the institution and to effectuate the guarantee under Article 30(1). The best possible way is to hold that as long as the minority educational institution permits admission of citizens belonging to the non-minority class to a reasonable extent based upon merit, it will not be an infraction of Article 29(2), even though the institution admits students of the minority group of its own choice for whom the institution was meant. What would be a reasonable extent would depend upon variable factors, and it may not be advisable to fix any specific percentage. The situation would vary according to the type of institution and the nature of education that is being imparted in the institution. Usually, at the school level, although it may be possible to fill up all the seats with students of the minority group, at the higher level, either in colleges or in technical institutions, it may not be possible to fill up all the seats with the students of the minority group. However, even if it is possible to fill up all the seats with students of the minority group, the moment the institution is granted aid, the institution will have to admit students of the non-minority group to a reasonable extent, whereby the character of the institution is not annihilated, and at the same time, the rights of the citizen engrafted under Article 29(2) are not subverted. It is for this reason that a variable percentage of admission of minority students depending on the type of institution and education is desirable, and indeed, necessary, to promote the constitutional guarantee enshrined in both Article 29(2) and Article 30.

Decision by Supreme Court:

Q.1. What is the meaning and content of the expression "minorities" in Article 30 of the Constitution of India?

A. Linguistic and religious minorities are covered by the expression "minority" under Article 30 of the Constitution. Since reorganisation of the State in India has been on linguistic lines, therefore, for the purpose of determining the minority the unit will be the State and note the whole of India. Thus, religious and linguistic minorities, who have been put at par in Article 30, have to be considered State-wise.

Q2 To what extent can professional education be treated as a matter coming under minorities rights under Article 30?

A. Article 30(1) gives religious and linguistic minorities the right to establish and administer educational institutions of their choice. The use of the words "of their choice" indicates that even professional educational institutions would be covered by Article 30.

Q.3 Whether the admission of students to minority educational institution, whether aided or unaided, can be regulated by the State Government or by the University to which the institution is affiliated?

A. Admission of students to unaided minority educational institutions, viz., schools and undergraduates colleges where the scope for merit-based selection is practically nil, cannot be regulated by the concerned State or University, except for providing the qualifications and minimum conditions of eligibility in the interest of academic standards.

The right to admit students being an essential facet of the right to administer educational institutions of their choice, as contemplated under Article 30 of the Constitution, the state government or the university may not be entitled to interfere with that right, so long as the admission to the unaided educational institutions is on a transparent basis and the merit is adequately taken care of. The right to administer, not being absolute, there could be regulatory measures for ensuring educational standards and maintaining excellence thereof, and it is more so in the matter of admissions to professional institutions.

A minority institution does not cease to be so, the moment grant-in-aid is received by the institution. An aided minority educational institution, therefore, would be entitled to have the right of admission of students belonging to the minority group and at the same time, would be required to admit a reasonable extent of non-minority students, so that the rights under Article 30(1) are not substantially impaired and further the citizens rights under Article 29(2) are not infringed. What would be a reasonable extent, would vary from the types of institution, the courses of education for which admission is being sought and other factors like educational needs. The concerned State Government has to notify the percentage of the non-minority students to be admitted in the light of the above observations. Observance of inter se merit amongst the applicants belonging to the minority group could be ensured. In the case of aided professional institutions, it can also be stipulated that passing of the common entrance test held by the state agency is necessary to seek admission. As regards non-minority students who are eligible to seek admission for the remaining seats, admission should normally be on the basis of the common entrance test held by the state agency followed by counselling wherever it exists.

Q4 Whether the minority's rights to establish and administer educational institutions of their choice will include the procedure and method of admission and selection of students?

A. A minority institution may have its own procedure and method of admission as well as selection of students, but such a procedure must be fair and transparent, and the selection of students in professional and higher education colleges should be on the basis of merit. The procedure adopted or selection made should not tantamount to mal-administration. Even an unaided minority institution ought not to ignore the merit of the students for admission, while exercising its right to admit students to the colleges aforesaid, as in that event, the institution will fail to achieve excellence.

Q5 Whether the minority institutions' right of admission of students and to lay down procedure and method of admission, if any, would be affected in any way by the receipt of State aid?

A. While giving aid to professional institutions, it would be permissible for the authority giving aid to prescribe by-rules or regulations, the conditions on the basis of which admission will be granted to different aided colleges by virtue of merit, coupled with the reservation policy of the state qua non-minority students. The merit may be determined either through a common entrance test conducted by the concerned University or the Government followed by counselling, or on the basis of an entrance test conducted by individual institutions--the method to be followed is for the university or the government to decide. The authority may also devise other means to ensure that admission is granted to an aided professional institution on the basis of merit. In the case of such institutions, it will be permissible for the government or the university to provide that consideration should be shown to the weaker sections of the society.

Q6 Whether the statutory provisions which regulate the facets of administration like control over educational agencies, control over governing bodies, conditions of affiliation including recognition/withdrawal thereof, and appointment of staff, employees, teachers and Principal including their service conditions and regulation of fees, etc. would interfere with the right of administration of minorities?

A. So far as the statutory provisions regulating the facets of administration are concerned, in case of an unaided minority educational institution, the regulatory measure of control should be minimal and the conditions of recognition as well as the conditions of affiliation to an university or board have to be complied with, but in the matter of day-to-day management like the appointment of staff, teaching and non-teaching, and administrative control over them, the management should have the freedom and there should not be any external controlling agency. However, a rational procedure for the selection of teaching staff and for taking disciplinary action has to be evolved by the management itself.

For redressing the grievances of employees of aided and unaided institutions who are subjected to punishment or termination from service, a mechanism will have to be evolved, and in our opinion, appropriate tribunals could be constituted, and till then, such tribunals could be presided over by a Judicial Officer of the rank of District Judge.

The State or other controlling authorities, however, can always prescribe the minimum qualification, experience and other conditions bearing on the merit of an individual for being appointed as a teacher or a principal of any educational institution.

Regulations can be framed governing service conditions for teaching and other staff for whom aid is provided by the state, without interfering with the overall administrative control of the management over the staff.

Fees to be charged by unaided institutions cannot be regulated but no institution should charge capitation fee.

Q.7 What is the meaning of the expressions "Education" and "Educational Institutions" in various provisions of the Constitution? Is the right to establish and administer educational institutions guaranteed under the Constitution?

A. The expression "education" in the Articles of the Constitution means and includes education at all levels from the primary school level upto the post-graduate level. It includes professional education. The expression "educational institutions" means institutions that impart education, where "education" is as understood hereinabove.

The right to establish and administer educational institutions is guaranteed under the Constitution to all citizens under Articles 19(1)(g) and 26, to minorities specifically under Article 30.

All citizens have a right to establish and administer educational institutions under Articles 19(1)(g) and 26, but this right is subject to the provisions of Articles 19(6) and 26(a). However, minority institutions will have a right to admit students belonging to the minority group.

Chapter-9

Extent to which State can Regulate Admissions made by unaided minority or non-minority Educational Institutions[156]

Facts in Nutshell

Education used to be charity or philanthropy in good old times. Gradually it became an 'occupation'. Some of the Judicial dicta go on to hold it as an 'industry'. Whether, to receive education, is a fundamental right[157] or not has been debated for quite some time. But it is settled that establishing and administering of an educational institution for imparting knowledge to the students is an occupation, protected by Article 19(1)(g)[158] and

---

156 Appellants: P.A. Inamdar and Ors. Vs. Respondent: State of Maharashtra and Ors.
Hon'ble Judges/Coram: R.C. Lahoti, C.J., Y.K. Sabharwal, D.M. Dharmadhikari, Arun Kumar, G.P. Mathur, Tarun Chatterjee and P.K. Balasubramanyan, JJ., Supreme Court of India
MANU/SC/0482/2005, Decided On: 12.08.2005
Hon'ble Judges/Coram:
R.C. Lahoti, C.J., Y.K. Sabharwal, D.M. Dharmadhikari, Arun Kumar, G.P. Mathur, Tarun Chatterjee and P.K. Balasubramanyan, JJ.

157 **Fundamental rights** are a group of rights that have been recognized by the Supreme Court as requiring a high degree of protection from government encroachment. These rights are specifically identified in the Constitution
(i.e. in the Bill of Rights), or have been found under Due Process.
Fundamental rights, the basic and civil liberties of the people, are protected under the charter of rights contained in Part III (Article 12 to 35) of the Constitution of India.

158 **Article 19 in The Constitution Of India 1949**
19. Protection of certain rights regarding freedom of speech etc
(1) All citizens shall have the right
(a) to freedom of speech and expression;
(b) to assemble peaceably and without arms;
(c) to form associations or unions;
(d) to move freely throughout the territory of India;
(e) to reside and settle in any part of the territory of India; and

116

additionally by Article 26(a)[159], if there is no element of profit generation. As of now, imparting education has come to be a means of livelihood for some professionals and a mission in life for some altruists.

Education has since long been a matter of litigation. Law reports are replete with rulings touching and centering around education in its several aspects. Until Pai Foundation, there were four oft quoted leading cases holding the field of education. They were Unni Krishnan v. State of Andhra

---

(f) omitted

(g) to practise any profession, or to carry on any occupation, trade or business

(2) Nothing in sub clause (a) of clause (1) shall affect the operation of any existing law, or prevent the State from making any law, in so far as such law imposes reasonable restrictions on the exercise of the right conferred by the said sub clause in the interests of the sovereignty and integrity of India, the security of the State, friendly relations with foreign States, public order, decency or morality or in relation to contempt of court, defamation or incitement to an offence

(3) Nothing in sub clause (b) of the said clause shall affect the operation of any existing law in so far as it imposes, or prevent the State from making any law imposing, in the interests of the sovereignty and integrity of India or public order, reasonable restrictions on the exercise of the right conferred by the said sub clause

(4) Nothing in sub clause (c) of the said clause shall affect the operation of any existing law in so far as it imposes, or prevent the State from making any law imposing, in the interests of the sovereignty and integrity of India or public order or morality, reasonable restrictions on the exercise of the right conferred by the said sub clause

(5) Nothing in sub clauses (d) and (e) of the said clause shall affect the operation of any existing law in so far as it imposes, or prevent the State from making any law imposing, reasonable restrictions on the exercise of any of the rights conferred by the said sub clauses either in the interests of the general public or for the protection of the interests of any Scheduled Tribe

(6) Nothing in sub clause (g) of the said clause shall affect the operation of any existing law in so far as it imposes, or prevent the State from making any law imposing, in the interests of the general public, reasonable restrictions on the exercise of the right conferred by the said sub clause, and, in particular, nothing in the said sub clause shall affect the operation of any existing law in so far as it relates to, or prevent the State from making any law relating to,

(i) the professional or technical qualifications necessary for practising any profession or carrying on any occupation, trade or business, or

(ii) the carrying on by the State, or by a corporation owned or controlled by the State, of any trade, business, industry or service, whether to the exclusion, complete or partial, of citizens or otherwise

159 **Article 26 in The Constitution Of India 1949**

26. Freedom to manage religious affairs Subject to public order, morality and health, every religious denomination or any section thereof shall have the right

(a) to establish and maintain institutions for religious and charitable purposes;

(b) to manage its own affairs in matters of religion;

(c) to own and acquire movable and immovable property; and

(d) to administer such property in accordance with law

Pradesh [1993] 1 SCR 594, St. Stephen's College v. University of Delhi AIR 1992 SC 1630, Ahmedabad St. Xavier's College Society v. State of Gujarat, [1975] 1 SCR 173 and In Re: Kerala Education Bill, 1957, (1958) SCR 995. For convenience sake, these cases will be referred to as Unni Krishnan, St. Stephen's, St. Xavier's and Kerala Education Bill respectively. All these cases amongst others came up for the consideration of Supreme Court in Pai Foundation.

"Education" was a State Subject in view of the following Entry 11 placed in List II - State List:-

"11. Education including universities, subject to the provisions of entries 63, 64, 65 and 66 of List I and entry 25 of List III."

By the Constitution (42nd Amendment) Act 1976, the abovesaid Entry was directed to be deleted and instead Entry 25 in List III - Concurrent List, was directed to be suitably amended so as to read as under:-

"25. Education, including technical education, medical education and universities, subject to the provisions of entries 63, 64, 65 and 66 of List I; vocational and technical training of labour."

Pai Foundation Judgment was delivered on 31.10.2002. The Union of India, various State Governments and the Educational Institutions, each understood the majority judgment in its own way. The State Governments embarked upon enacting laws and framing the regulations, governing the educational institutions in consonance with their own understanding of Pai Foundation. This led to litigation in several Courts. Interim orders passed therein by High Courts came to be challenged before Supreme Court. At the hearing, again the parties through their learned counsel tried to interpret the majority decision in Pai Foundation in different ways as it suited them. The parties agreed that there were certain anomalies and doubts, calling for clarification. The persons seeking such clarifications were unaided professional educational institutions, both minority and non-minority. The Court formulated four questions as arising for consideration in Islamic Foundation case[160]:

(1) whether the educational institutions are entitled to fix their own fee structure;

(2) whether minority and non-minority educational institutions stand on

---

160 CASE NO.:
   Writ Petition (civil) 350 of 1993

the same footing and have the same rights;

(3) whether private unaided professional colleges are entitled to fill in their seats, to the extent of 100%, and if not, to what extent; and

(4) whether private unaided professional colleges are entitled to admit students by evolving their own method of admission.

The gist of the answers given by the Constitution Bench of the Court as under:

(1) Each minority institution is entitled to have its own fee structure subject to the condition that there can be no profiteering and capitation fees cannot be charged. A provision for reasonable surplus can be made to enable future expansion. The relevant factors which would go into determining the reasonability of a fee structure, in the opinion of majority, are: (i) the infrastructure and facilities available, (ii) the investments made, (iii) salaries paid to the teachers and staff, (iv) future plans for expansion and betterment of the institution etc.

(2) Minority institutions stand on a better footing than non-minority institutions. Minority educational institutions have a guarantee or assurance to establish and administer educational institutions of their choice. State Legislation, primary or delegated, cannot favour non- minority institution over minority institution. The difference arises because of Article 30, the protection whereunder is available to minority educational institutions only. The majority opinion called it a "special right" given under Article 30[161].

Minority educational institutions do not have a higher right in terms of Article 30(1); the rights of minorities and non-minorities are equal. What is conferred by Article 30(1) of the Constitution is "certain additional protection" with the object of bringing the minorities on the same

---

161 **Article 30 in The Constitution Of India 1949**
30. Right of minorities to establish and administer educational institutions
(1) All minorities, whether based on religion or language, shall have the right to establish and administer educational institutions of their choice
(1A) In making any law providing for the compulsory acquisition of any property of an educational institution established and administered by a minority, referred to in clause (1), the State shall ensure that the amount fixed by or determined under such law for the acquisition of such property is such as would not restrict or abrogate the right guaranteed under that clause
(2) The state shall not, in granting aid to educational institutions, discriminate against any educational institution on the ground that it is under the management of a minority, whether based on religion or language

platform as that of non-minorities, so that the minorities are protected by establishing and administering educational institutions for the benefit of their own community, whether based on religion or language.

However, the majority opinion in Islamic Academy has by explaining Pai Foundation held as under:

(1) In professional institutions, as they are unaided, there will be full autonomy in their administration, but the principle of merit cannot be sacrificed, as excellence in profession is in national interest.

(2) Without interfering with the autonomy of unaided institutions, the object of merit based admissions can be secured by insisting on it as a condition to the grant of recognition and subject to the recognition of merit, the management can be given certain discretion in admitting students.

(3) The management can have quota for admitting students at its discretion but subject to satisfying the test of merit based admissions, which can be achieved by allowing management to pick up students of their own choice from out of those who have passed the common entrance test conducted by a centralized mechanism. Such common entrance test can be conducted by the State or by an association of similarly placed institutions in the State.

(4) The State can provide for reservation in favour of financially or socially backward sections of the society.

(5) The prescription for percentage of seats, that is allotment of different quotas such as management seats, State's quota, appropriated by the State for allotment to reserved categories etc., has to be done by the State in accordance with the "local needs" and the interests/needs of that minority community in the State, both deserving paramount consideration. The exact concept of "local needs" is not clarified. The plea that each minority unaided educational institution can hold its own admission test was expressly overruled. The principal consideration which prevailed with the majority in Islamic Academy for holding in favour of common entrance test was to avoid great hardship and incurring of huge cost by the hapless students in appearing for individual tests of various colleges.

Not clear with the above PAI judgment and Islamic Academy Judgment the aggrieved persons were before court i.e. unaided minority and non-minority institutions imparting professional education.

Question before the Supreme Court

The issues arising for decision before court are:

120

(1) To what extent the State can regulate the admissions made by unaided (minority or non- minority) educational institutions? Can the State enforce its policy of reservation and/or appropriate to itself any quota in admissions to such institutions?

(2) Whether unaided (minority and non-minority) educational institutions are free to devise their own admission procedure or whether direction made in Islamic Academy for compulsorily holding entrance test by the State or association of institutions and to choose therefrom the students entitled to admission in such institutions, can be sustained in light of the law laid down in Pai Foundation?

(3) Whether Islamic Academy could have issued guidelines in the matter of regulating the fee payable by the students to the educational institutions?

(4) Can the admission procedure and fee structure be regulated or taken over by the Committees ordered to be constituted by Islamic Academy?

Contention by the learned counsel for the appellant:

Establishing and running an educational institution is a guaranteed fundamental right of 'occupation' under Article 19(1)(g) of the Constitution. Article 19(6) permits State to make regulations and place reasonable restrictions in public interest upon the rights enjoyed by citizens under Article 19(1)(g) of the Constitution. Any imposition of a system of selection of students for admission would be unreasonable if it deprives the private unaided institutions of the right of rational selection which it has devised for itself. Subject to the minimum qualifications that may be prescribed and to some system of computing the equivalence between different kinds of qualifications like a common entrance test, it can evolve a system of selection involving both written and oral tests based on principle of fairness.

The State can prescribe minimum qualifications and may prescribe systems of computing equivalence in ascertaining merit; however, the right of rational selection, which would necessarily involve the right to decide upon the method by which a particular institution computes such equivalence, is protected by Article 19 and infringement of this right constitutes an unreasonable encroachment upon the constitutionally guaranteed autonomy of such institutions.

It was further argued that where States take over the right of the institution to grant admission and/or to fix the fees, it constitutes nationalization of educational institutions. Such nationalization of education is an unreasonable restriction on the right conferred under Article 19.

It was argued that State necessity cannot be a ground to curtail the right of a citizen conferred under Article 19(1)(g) of the Constitution. The Constitution casts a duty upon the States to provide educational facilities. The State is obliged to carry out this duty from revenue raised by the State. The shortfall in the efforts of the State is met by the private enterprise, that however, does not entitle the State to nationalize, whether in the whole or in part, such private enterprise.

Learned counsel in elaborating his argument tried to make a distinction between the rights of aided institutions and unaided institutions. Article 29(2) places a limitation on the right of an aided institution by providing that if State aid is obtained, 'no citizen shall be denied admission on grounds only of religion, race, caste, language or any of them'. It was submitted that as a necessary corollary, no such limitation can be placed while regulating admission in an unaided minority institution which may prefer to admit students of minority community. So far as unaided minority educational institutions are concerned, the submission made is that government has no right or power, much less duty, to decide as to which method of selection of students is to be adopted by minority institutions. The role of the government is confined to ensuring that there is no mal-administration in the name of selection of students or in the fixation of fees. No doubt, the State is under a duty to prevent mal-administration, that is to control charging of capitation fees for the seats regardless of merit and commercializing education resulting in exploitation of students, but to prevent mal- administration of the above nature or on the ground that there is likelihood of such mal-administration, the State cannot take over the administration of the institutions themselves into its own hands. The likelihood of an abuse of a constitutional right cannot ever furnish justification for a denial of that right. An apprehension that a citizen may abuse his liberty does not provide justification for imposing restraints on the liberty of citizens. Similarly, the apprehension that the minorities may abuse their educational rights under Article 30 of the Constitution cannot constitute a valid basis for the State to take over those rights.

Contention by the learned counsel for the unaided private professional colleges

On behalf of unaided private professional colleges, learned counsel further submitted that there are many private educational institutes which have been set up by people belonging to a region or a community or a class in order to promote their own groups. As long as these groups form an unaided minority institution, they are entitled to have transparent criteria to admit students belonging to their group. For instance, scheduled castes and scheduled tribes have started Ambedkar Medical College; Lingayaths have started KLE Medical College in Belgaun and people belonging to Vokalliga community have started Kempegowda Medical College. Similarly, Edava community in Kerala has started its own colleges. Sugar cooperatives in Maharashtra have started their own colleges. Learned counsel also highlighted an instance of a college opened in Tamil Nadu by State Transport Workers for the education of their children on the engineering side. He submitted that if the State is allowed to interfere in the admission procedure in these private institutions set up with the object of providing educational facilities to their own group, community or poorer sections, the very purpose and object of setting up a private medical college by a group or community for their own people would be defeated.

According to learned counsel, the State control in unaided private professional colleges can only be to the extent of monitoring or overseeing its working so that they do not indulge in profiteering by charging capitation fees and sacrifice merit. It was argued as to why private professional institutes should not be allowed to modernize its facilities and provide better professional education than government institutes.

Education

(i) What is 'education'? (ii) What is the inter-relationship of Articles 19(1) (g), 29 and 30 of the Constitution? (iii) In the context of minority educational institutions, what difference does it make if they are aided or unaided or if they seek recognition or affiliation or do not do so? (iv) Would it make any difference if the instructions imparted in such educational institutions relate to professional or non-professional courses of study?

Education

'Education' according to Chambers Dictionary is "bringing up or training; strengthening of the powers of body or mind; culture."

In Advanced Law Lexicon (P. Ramanatha Aiyar, 3rd Edition, 2005, Vol.2) 'education' is defined in very wide terms. It is stated : "Education is the bringing up; the process of developing and training the powers and capabilities of human beings. In its broadest sense the word comprehends not merely the instruction received at school, or college but the whole course of training moral, intellectual and physical; is not limited to the ordinary instruction of the child in the pursuits of literature. It also comprehends a proper attention to the moral and religious sentiments of the child. And it is sometimes used as synonymous with 'learning.'"

In The Sole Trustee, Lok Shikshana Trust v. C.I.T., [1975]101 ITR 234 (SC), the term 'education' was held to mean - "the systematic instruction, schooling or training given to the young in preparation for the work of life. It also connotes the whole course of scholastic instruction which a person has received. What education connotes is the process of training and developing the knowledge, skill, mind and character of students by formal schooling."

In 'India - Vision 2020' published by Planning Commission of India, it is stated (at p.250) - "Education is an important input both for the growth of the society as well as for the individual. Properly planned educational input can contribute to increase in the Gross National Products, cultural richness, build positive attitude towards technology and increase efficiency and effectiveness of the governance. Education opens new horizons for an individual, provides new aspirations and develops new values. It strengthens competencies and develops commitment. Education generates in an individual a critical outlook on social and political realities and sharpens the ability to self-examination, self-monitoring and self-criticism."

"The term 'Knowledge Society', 'Information Society' and 'Learning Society' have now become familiar expressions in the educational parlance, communicating emerging global trends with far-reaching implications for growth and development of any society. These are not to be seen as mere chichi or fads but words that are pregnant with unimaginable potentialities. Information revolution, information technologies and knowledge industries, constitute important dimensions of an information society and contribute effectively to the growth of a knowledge society." (ibid, p.246)

"Alvin Toffler (1980) has advanced the idea that power at the dawn of civilization resided in the 'muscle'. Power then got associated with money and in 20th century it shifted its focus to 'mind'. Thus the shift from physical power to wealth power to mind power is an evolution in the shifting foundations of economy. This shift supports the observation of Francis Bacon who said 'knowledge itself is power'; stressing the same point and upholding the supremacy of mind power, in his characteristic expression, Winston Churchill said, "the Empires of the future shall be empires of the mind". Thus, he corroborated Bacon and professed the emergence of the knowledge society." (ibid, p.247)

According to Dr. Zakir Hussain, a great statesman with democratic credentials, a secularist and an educationist, a true democracy is one where each and every citizen is involved in the democratic process and this end cannot be achieved unless we remove the prevailing large-scale illiteracy in our country. Unless universal education is achieved which allows every citizen to participate actively in the processes of democracy, we can never claim to be a true democracy. Dr. Zakir Hussain sought to ensure that the seeds of knowledge were germinated in the minds of as many citizens as possible, with a view to enabling them to perform their assigned roles on the stage of democracy[162].

Under Article 41[163] of the Constitution, right to education, amongst others, is obligated to be secured by the State by making effective provision therefore.

Fundamental duties[164] recognized by Article 51A[165] include, amongst

---

162 [Dr. Zakir Hussain, as quoted by Justice A.M. Ahmadi, the then Chief Justice of India, (1996) 2 SCC (J) 1

163 **Article 41 in The Constitution Of India 1949**
41. Right to work, to education and to public assistance in certain cases The State shall, within the limits of its economic capacity and development, make effective provision for securing the right to work, to education and to public assistance in cases of unemployment, old age, sickness and disablement, and in other cases of undeserved want

164 The **Fundamental Duties** are moral obligations on all citizens of India which help promote a spirit of patriotism and uphold the unity, integrity and sovereignty of India. These **duties**, given in Part IV–A of the Constitution of India, concern the self, the environment, the State and society and the Nation.

165 **Article 51A in The Constitution Of India 1949**
51A. Fundamental duties It shall be the duty of every citizen of India (a) to abide by the Constitution and respect its ideals and institutions, the national Flag and the National Anthem;
(b) to cherish and follow the noble ideals which inspired our national struggle for freedom;
(c) to uphold and protect the sovereignty, unity and integrity of India;
(d) to defend the country and render national service when called upon to do so;
(e) to promote harmony and the spirit of common brotherhood amongst all the people of India transcending religious, linguistic and regional or sectional diversities; to renounce practices derogatory to the dignity of women;
(f) to value and preserve the rich heritage of our composite culture;
(g) to protect and improve the natural environment including forests, lakes, rivers and wild life, and to have compassion for living creatures;
(h) to develop the scientific temper, humanism and the spirit of inquiry and reform;
(i) to safeguard public property and to abjure violence;
(j) to strive towards excellence in all spheres of individual and collective activity so that

others, (i) to develop the scientific temper, humanism and the spirit of inquiry and reform; and (ii) to strive towards excellence in all spheres of individual and collective activity so that the nation constantly rises to higher levels of endeavour and achievement. None can be achieved or ensured except by means of education. It is well accepted by the thinkers, philosophers and academicians that if JUSTICE, LIBERTY, EQUALITY and FRATERNITY[166], including social, economic and political justice, the golden goals set out in the Preamble to the Constitution of India are to be achieved, the Indian polity has to be educated and educated with excellence. Education is a national wealth which must be distributed equally and widely, as far as possible, in the interest of creating an egalitarian society, to enable the country to rise high and face global competition. 'Tireless striving stretching its arms towards perfection' (to borrow the expression from Rabindranath Tagore) would not be successful unless strengthened by education.

Education is "...continual growth of personality, steady development of character, and the qualitative improvement of life. A trained mind has the capacity to draw spiritual nourishment from every experience, be it defeat or victory, sorrow or joy. Education is training the mind and not stuffing the brain.[167]"

"We want that education by which character is formed, strength of mind is increased, the intellect is expanded, and by which one can stand on one's own feet." "The end of all education, all training, should be man-making. The end and aim of all training is to make the man grow. The training by which the current and expression of will are brought under control and become fruitful is called education.[168]"

Education, accepted as a useful activity, whether for charity or for profit, is an occupation. Nevertheless, it does not cease to be a service to the society. And even though an occupation, it cannot be equated to a trade or a business.

In short, education is national wealth essential for the nation's progress and prosperity.

---

the nation constantly rises to higher levels of endeavour and achievement

166 **Meaning of Fraternity:**
   A body of people united in interests, aims, etc

167 (See Eternal Values for A Changing Society, Vol. III Education for Human Excellence, published by Bharatiya Vidya Bhavan, Bombay, at p. 19)

168 (Swami Vivekanand as quoted in ibid, at p.20)

The right to establish an educational institution, for charity or for profit, being an occupation, is protected by Article 19(1) (g):

Notwithstanding the fact that the right of a minority to establish and administer an educational institution would be protected by Article 19(1)(g) yet the Founding Fathers of the Constitution felt the need of enacting Article 30. The reasons are too obvious to require elaboration. Article 30(1) is intended to instill confidence in minorities against any executive or legislative encroachment on their right to establish and administer educational institution of their choice. Article 30(1) though styled as a right, is more in the nature of protection for minorities. But for Article 30, an educational institution, even though based on religion or language, could have been controlled or regulated by law enacted under Clause (6) of Article 19, and so, Article 30 was enacted as a guarantee to the minorities that so far as the religious or linguistic minorities are concerned, educational institutions of their choice will enjoy protection from such legislation. However, such institutions cannot be discriminated against by the State solely on account of their being minority institutions. The minorities being numerically less qua non-minorities, may not be able to protect their religion or language and such cultural values and their educational institutions will be protected under Article 30, at the stage of law making. However, merely because Article 30(1) has been enacted, minority educational institutions do not become immune from the operation of regulatory measure because the right to administer does not include the right to mal-administer. To what extent the State regulation can go, is the issue. The real purpose sought to be achieved by Article 30 is to give minorities some additional protection. Once aided, the autonomy conferred by the protection of Article 30(1) on the minority educational institution is diluted as provisions of Article 29(2) will be attracted. Certain conditions in the nature of regulations can legitimately accompany the State aid.

As an occupation, right to impart education is a fundamental right under Article 19(1)(g) and, therefore, subject to control by clause (6) of Article 19. This right is available to all citizens without drawing a distinction between minority and non- minority. Such a right is, generally speaking, subject to laws imposing reasonable restrictions in the interest of the general public. In particular, laws may be enacted on the following subjects: (i) the professional or technical qualifications necessary for practicing any profession or carrying on any occupation, trade or business; (ii) the carrying on by the State, or by a corporation owned or controlled by the

State of any trade, business, industry or service whether to the exclusion, complete or partial of citizens or otherwise. Care is taken of minorities, religious or linguistic, by protecting their right to establish and administer educational institutions of their choice under Article 30. To some extent, what may be permissible by way of restriction under Article 19(6) may fall foul of Article 30. This is the additional protection which Article 30(1) grants to the minorities.

The employment of expressions 'right to establish and administer' and 'educational institution of their choice' in Article 30(1) gives the right a very wide amplitude. Therefore, a minority educational institution has a right to admit students of its own choice, it can, as a matter of its own freewill, admit students of non-minority community. However, non-minority students cannot be forced upon it. The only restriction on the freewill of the minority educational institution admitting students belonging to non-minority community is, as spelt out by Article 30 itself, that the manner and number of such admissions should not be violative of the minority character of the institution.

'Minority' And 'Minority Educational Institutions':

The term 'minority' is not defined in the Constitution. Chief Justice Kirpal, speaking for the majority in Pai Foundation, took clue from the provisions of the State Reorganisation Act and held that in view of India having been divided into different linguistic States, carved out on the basis of the language of the majority of persons of that region, it is the State, and not the whole of India, that shall have to be taken as the unit for determining linguistic minority viz-a-viz Article 30. Inasmuch as Article 30(1) places on par religions and languages, he held that the minority status, whether by reference to language or by reference to religion, shall have to be determined by treating the State as unit. The principle would remain the same whether it is a Central legislation or a State legislation dealing with linguistic or religious minority. Ruma Pal, J. defined the word 'minority' to mean 'numerically less'. However, she refused to take the State as a unit for the purpose of determining minority status as, in her opinion, the question of minority status must be determined with reference to the country as a whole. She assigned reasons for the purpose. Needless to say, her opinion is a lone voice. Thus, with the dictum of Pai Foundation, it cannot be doubted that minority, whether linguistic or religious, is determinable only by reference to the demography of a State and not by taking into consideration the population of the country as a whole.

Such definition of minority resolves one issue but gives rise to many a questions when it comes to defining 'minority educational institution'. Whether a minority educational institution, though established by a minority, can cater to the needs of that minority only? Can there be an enquiry to identify the person or persons who have really established the institution? Can a minority institution provide cross-border or inter-State educational facilities and yet retain the character of minority educational institution?

In Kerala Education Bill, the scope and ambit of right conferred by Article 30(1) came up for consideration. Article 30(1) does not require that minorities based on religion should establish educational institutions for teaching religion only or that linguistic minority should establish educational institution for teaching its language only. The object underlying Article 30(1) is to see the desire of minorities being fulfilled that their children should be brought up properly and efficiently and acquire eligibility for higher university education and go out in the world fully equipped with such intellectual attainments as will make them fit for entering public services, educational institutions imparting higher instructions including general secular education. Thus, the twin objects sought to be achieved by Article 30(1) in the interest of minorities are: (i) to enable such minority to conserve its religion and language, and (ii) to give a thorough, good general education to the children belonging to such minority. So long as the institution retains its minority character by achieving and continuing to achieve the above said two objectives, the institution would remain a minority institution.

Minority educational institutions: classifiable in three:

To establish an educational institution is a Fundamental Right. Several educational institutions have come up. In Kerala Education Bill, 'minority educational institutions' came to be classified into three categories, namely, (i) those which do not seek either aid or recognition from the State; (ii) those which want aid; and (iii) those which want only recognition but not aid. It was held that the first category protected by Article 30(1) can "exercise that right to their hearts' content" unhampered by restrictions. The second category is most significant. Most of the educational institutions would fall in that category as no educational institution can, in modern times, afford to subsist and efficiently function without some State aid. So is with the third category. An educational institution may survive without aid but would still stand in need of recognition because in the absence of recognition, education imparted therein may not really serve the purpose as for want of recognition the students passing out from such educational institutions may not be entitled to admission in other educational institutions for higher studies and may also not be eligible for securing jobs. Once an educational institution is granted aid or aspires for recognition, the State may grant aid or recognition accompanied by certain restrictions or conditions which must be followed as essential to the grant of such aid or recognition. Supreme Court clarified in Kerala Educational Bill[169] that 'the right to establish and administer educational institutions' conferred by Article 30(1) does not include the right to mal-administer, and that is very obvious. Merely because an educational institution belongs to minority it cannot ask for aid or recognition though running in unhealthy surroundings, without any competent teachers and which does not maintain even a fair standard of teaching or which teaches matters subversive to the welfare of the scholars. Therefore, the State may prescribe reasonable regulations to ensure the excellence of the educational institutions to be granted aid or to be recognized. To wit, it is open to the State to lay down conditions for recognition such as, an institution must have a particular amount of funds or properties or number of students or standard of education and so on. The dividing line is that in the name of laying down conditions for aid or recognition the State cannot directly or indirectly defeat the very protection conferred by Article 30(1) on the minority to establish and administer educational institutions.

Difference between professional and non-professional education institutions

Dealing with unaided minority educational institutions, Pai Foundation holds that Article 30 does not come in the way of the State stepping in for the purpose of securing transparency and recognition of merit in the matter of admissions. Regulatory measures for ensuring educational standards and maintaining excellence thereof are no anathema to the protection conferred by Article 30(1). However, a distinction is to be drawn between unaided minority educational institution of the level of schools and undergraduate colleges on one side and the institutions of higher education, in particular, those imparting professional education on the other side. In the former, the scope for merit based selection is practically nil and hence may not call for regulation. But in the case of latter, transparency and merit have to be unavoidably taken care of and cannot be compromised. There could be regulatory measures for ensuring educational standards and maintaining

---

169 In Re: Kerala Education Bill, 1957 (1958) SCR 995

excellence thereof[170].

Educational institutions imparting higher education, i.e. graduate level and above and in particular specialized education such as technical or professional, constitutes a separate class. While embarking upon resolving issues of constitutional significance, where the letter of the Constitution is not clear, we have to keep in view the spirit of the Constitution, as spelt out by its entire scheme. Education aimed at imparting professional or technical qualifications stand on a different footing from other educational instruction. Apart from other provisions, Article 19(6) is a clear indicator and so are clauses (h) and (j) of Article 51A. Education upto undergraduate level aims at imparting knowledge just to enrich mind and shape the personality of a student. Graduate level study is a doorway to admissions in educational institutions imparting professional or technical or other higher education and, therefore, at that level, the considerations akin to those relevant for professional or technical educational institutions step in and become relevant. This is in national interest and strengthening the national wealth, education included. Education up to undergraduate level on one hand and education at graduate and post-graduate levels and in professional and technical institutions on the other are to be treated on different levels. A number of legislations occupying the field of education whose constitutional validity has been tested and accepted suggest that while recognition or affiliation may not be a must for education up to undergraduate level or, even if required, may be granted as a matter of routine, recognition or affiliation is a must and subject to rigorous scrutiny when it comes to educational institutions awarding degrees, graduate or post-graduate, post-graduate diplomas and degrees in technical or professional disciplines.

In professional unaided institutions, the management will have the right to select teachers as per the qualifications and eligibility conditions laid down by the State/university subject to adoption of a rational procedure of selection. A rational fee structure should be adopted by the management, which would not be entitled to charge a capitation fee. Appropriate machinery can be devised by the State or university to ensure that no capitation fee is charged and that there is no profiteering, though a reasonable surplus for the furtherance of education is permissible. Conditions granting recognition or affiliation can broadly cover academic and educational matters including the welfare of students and teachers.

---

170 (See para 161, Answer to Q.4, in Pai Foundation)

It is well established all over the world that those who seek professional education must pay for it. The number of seats available in government and government-aided colleges is very small, compared to the number of persons seeking admission to the medical and engineering colleges. All those eligible and deserving candidates who could not be accommodated in government colleges would stand deprived of professional education. This void in the field of medical and technical education has been filled by institutions that are established in different places with the aid of donations and the active part taken by public-minded individuals. The object of establishing an institution has thus been to provide technical or professional education to the deserving candidates, and is not necessarily a commercial venture. In order that this intention is meaningful, the institution must be recognized. At the school level, the recognition or affiliation has to be sought from the educational authority or the body that conducts the school-leaving examination. It is only on the basis of that examination that a school-leaving certificate is granted, which enables a student to seek admission in further courses of study after school. A college or a professional educational institution has to get recognition from the university concerned, which normally requires certain conditions to be fulfilled before recognition. It has been held that conditions of affiliation or recognition, which pertain to the academic and educational character of the institution and ensure uniformity, efficiency and excellence in educational courses are valid, and that they do not violate even the provisions of Article 30 of the Constitution; but conditions that are laid down for granting recognition should not be such as may lead to governmental control of the administration of the private educational institutions.

Decision by Supreme Court

Unaided educational institutions; appropriation of quota by State and enforcement of reservation policy

(i) Minority educational institution, unaided and unrecognized

Pai Foundation is unanimous on the view that the right to establish and administer an institution, the phrase as employed in Article 30(1) of the Constitution, comprises of the following rights: (a) to admit students; (b) to set up a reasonable fee structure; (c) to constitute a governing body; (d) to appoint staff (teaching and non-teaching); and (e) to take action if there is dereliction of duty on the part of any of the employees.

A minority educational institution may choose not to take any aid from the State and may also not seek any recognition or affiliation. It may be imparting such instructions and may have students learning such knowledge that do not stand in need of any recognition. Such institutions would be those where instructions are imparted for the sake of instructions and learning is only for the sake of learning and acquiring knowledge. Obviously, such institutions would fall in the category of those who would exercise their right under the protection and privilege conferred by Article 30(1) "to their hearts content" unhampered by any restrictions excepting those which are in national interest based on considerations such as public safety, national security and national integrity or are aimed at preventing exploitation of students or teaching community. Such institutions cannot indulge in any activity which is violative of any law of the land.

They are free to admit all students of their own minority community if they so choose to do.

(ii) Minority unaided educational institutions asking for affiliation or recognition

Affiliation or recognition by the State or the Board or the University competent to do so, cannot be denied solely on the ground that the institution is a minority educational institution. However, the urge or need for affiliation or recognition brings in the concept of regulation by way of laying down conditions consistent with the requirement of ensuring merit, excellence of education and preventing mal-administration. For example, provisions can be made indicating the quality of the teachers by prescribing the minimum qualifications that they must possess and the courses of studies and curricula. The existence of infrastructure sufficient for its growth can be stipulated as a pre-requisite to the grant of recognition or affiliation. However, there cannot be interference in the day-to-day administration. The essential ingredients of the management, including admission of students, recruiting of staff and the quantum of fee to be charged, cannot be regulated.

Apart from the generalized position of law that right to administer does not include right to mal-administer, an additional source of power to regulate by enacting condition accompanying affiliation or recognition exists. Balance has to be struck between the two objectives: (i) that of ensuring the standard of excellence of the institution, and (ii) that of preserving the right of the minority to establish and administer its educational institution. Subject to reconciliation of the two objectives, any regulation accompanying affiliation or recognition must satisfy the triple tests: (i) the test of reasonableness and rationality, (ii) the test that the regulation would be conducive to making the institution an effective vehicle of education for the minority community or other persons who resort to it, and (iii) that there is no in-road on the protection conferred by Article 30(1) of the Constitution, that is, by framing the regulation the essential character of the institution being a minority educational institution, is not taken away.

(iii) Minority educational institutions receiving State aid

Conditions which can normally be permitted to be imposed on the educational institutions receiving the grant must be related to the proper utilization of the grant and fulfillment of the objectives.

The State cannot insist on private educational institutions which receive no aid from the State to implement State's policy on reservation for granting admission on lesser percentage of marks, i.e. on any criterion except merit. Unaided institutions, as they are not deriving any aid from State funds, can have their own admissions if fair, transparent, non-exploitative and based on merit.

Neither the policy of reservation can be enforced by the State nor any quota or percentage of admissions can be carved out to be appropriated by the State in a minority or non-minority unaided educational institution. Minority institutions are free to admit students of their own choice including students of non-minority community as also members of their own community from other States, both to a limited extent only and not in a manner and to such an extent that their minority educational institution status is lost. If they do so, they lose the protection of Article 30(1).

Admission procedure of unaided Educational Institutions.

So far as the minority unaided institutions are concerned to admit students being one of the components of "right to establish and administer an institution", the State cannot interfere therewith. Upto the level of undergraduate education, the minority unaided educational institutions enjoy total freedom.

However, different considerations would apply for graduate and post-graduate level of education, as also for technical and professional educational institutions. Such education cannot be imparted by any institution unless recognized by or affiliated with any competent authority created by law, such as a University, Board, Central or State Government or the like. Excellence in education and maintenance of high standards at this level are a must. To fulfill these objectives, the State can and rather must, in national interest, step in. The education, knowledge and learning at this level possessed by individuals collectively constitutes national wealth.

All institutions imparting same or similar professional education can join together for holding a common entrance test. The State can also provide a procedure of holding a common entrance test in the interest of securing fair and merit-based admissions and preventing mal-administration.

Having regard to the larger interest and welfare of the student community to promote merit, achieve excellence and curb mal-practices, it would be permissible to regulate admissions by providing a centralized and single window procedure. Such a procedure, to a large extent, can secure grant of merit based admissions on a transparent basis. Till regulations are framed, the admission committees can oversee admissions so as to ensure that merit is not the casualty.

Fee Regulations

To set up a reasonable fee structure is also a component of "the right to establish and administer an institution" within the meaning of Article 30(1) of the Constitution, as per the law declared in Pai Foundation. Every institution is free to devise its own fee structure subject to the limitation that there can be no profiteering and no capitation fee can be charged directly or indirectly.

Capitation Fees

Capitation fee cannot be permitted to be charged and no seat can be permitted to be appropriated by payment of capitation fee. 'Profession' has to be distinguished from 'business' or a mere 'occupation'. While in business, and to a certain extent in occupation, there is a profit motive, profession is primarily a service to society wherein earning is secondary or incidental. A student who gets a professional degree by payment of capitation fee, once qualified as a professional, is likely to aim more at earning rather than serving and that becomes a bane to the society. The charging of capitation fee by unaided minority and non-minority institutions for professional courses is just not permissible. Similarly, profiteering is also not permissible. Despite the legal position, Court cannot shut its eyes to the hard realities of commercialization of education and evil practices being adopted by many institutions to earn large amounts for their private or selfish ends. If capitation fee and profiteering is to be checked, the method of admission has to be regulated so that the admissions are based on merit and transparency and the students are not exploited. It is permissible to regulate admission and fee structure for achieving the purpose just stated.

Every institution is free to devise its own fee structure but the same can be regulated in the interest of preventing profiteering. No capitation fee can be charged.

Chapter-10

Conclusion

In the last 75 years of Independence women in India have gained entry in all spheres of public life. They have also been representing people at grass root democracy. They are now employed as drivers of heavy transport vehicles, conductors of services carriage, pilots etc. All women can be seen to be occupying class IV posts, to the post of a Chief Executive Officer of a Multinational company and they are now widely accepted in both police and army services yet they face discrimination.

The categorization on the basis of sex is in violation of the fundamental right to equality of opportunity and it is the fundamental duty of the State to protect against discrimination on the ground of sex in respect of institutions run by the State.

Instead of putting curbs on women's freedom, empowerment would be a more tenable and socially wise approach. This empowerment should reflect in the law enforcement strategies of the state as well as law modelling done in this behalf.

India is one the rare countries where in Sainik Schools and Rashtriya Military Schools only allows boys/males[171] for admission and no girls/females are allowed in them. It is pertinent to mention here that the role of Sainik Schools and Rashtriya Military Schools is such that without the admission of **Girls/ Females** it is unlikely that the mission of the schools for which it was conceived with the motive of bringing public school education to the door step of the common man and sending a maximum number of its cadets to National Defence Academy will be fulfilled as required.

---

171 Now this condition is changed and even girls are allowed in Sainik Schools and Rashtriya Military Schools after the Hon'ble Supreme Court Order

After NDA, Supreme Court Permits Girls To Appear For Military Schools Entrance For 2022 Term[172]

The **Supreme Court** directed the Centre to make arrangements for the induction of girls into the **Rashtriya Indian Military College** (RIMC) by allowing them to appear for the upcoming examination on **December 18, 2021** for the term beginning from **June 2022**. The Centre was directed to issue fresh advertisements in this regard.

Admission To RIMC

"Admission to RIMC is done through an All India Competetive examination held biannually in June and December every year for admission in January and July. All states of the union is allotted one seat while Maharashtra, Tamil Nadu and West Bengal allotted two seats, UP allotted three seats," Army Training Command had submitted in their affidavit.

On the aspect of gradual process to be followed in RIMC affidavit stated that, *"Increase capacity from 250 to 300 incrementally by inducting 05 girls per six months. The girls will be allowed to take the RIMC entrance examination scheduled in June 2022 for entry into RIMC for the term starting in January 2023."*

The affidavit further said that in Phase 2 there is a plan to increase capacity from 300 to 350 and to Induct 10 girls every month and at the end of that expansion, RIMC will have 250 boys and 100 girls and for this girls will be allowed to take the RIMC entrance examination scheduled in June 2027 for the term starting Jan 2028.

Admission to RMC

With regards to the admission in RMC, the affidavit stated that in the first phase, there would be reservation of 10% of total vacancies in each school for girl candidates for entry into class VI from the academic session 2022-23 and in the second phase, 10% seats will be reserved in each school for girl candidates for entry into class VI and class IX.

In so far as Sainik Schools are concerned, the Bench had on an earlier occasion made note of the Union of India's affidavit which stated that the process of admitting girls have already started and will be further expanded.

172https://www.livelaw.in/top-stories/supreme-court-permits-girls-to-appear-for-military-schools-entrance-for-2022-term-nda-183311

ITEM NO.11   COURT NO.6   SECTION PIL-W

S U P R E M E   C O U R T   O F   I N D I A
RECORD OF PROCEEDINGS

Writ Petition(s)(Civil) No.1416/2020

KUSH KALRA   Petitioner(s)

VERSUS

UNION OF INDIA & ORS.   Respondent(s)
(IA No. 6976/2022 - EXEMPTION FROM FILING AFFIDAVIT
  IA No. 87814/2021 - STAY APPLICATION)
WITH
W.P.(C) No. 524/2021 (PIL-W)
(I. A. No. 106572/2021- Application for permission)
Date : 08-03-2022 These matters were called on for hearing today.

CORAM :   HON'BLE MR. JUSTICE SANJAY KISHAN KAUL
          HON'BLE MR. JUSTICE M.M. SUNDRESH

For Petitioner(s) Petitioner-in-person
          Mr. Chinmoy Pradip Sharma, Sr .Adv.
          Mr. Mohit Paul, AOR
          Mr. Irfan Haseib, Adv.
          Mr. Bikram Dwivedi, Adv.
For Respondent(s) Ms. Aishwarya Bhati, ASG
          Ms. Ruchi Kohli, Adv.
          Ms. Archana Pathak Dave, Adv.
          Mr. Chinmayee Chandra, Adv.
          Mr. Nitin Pavuluri, Adv.
          Mr. Ameya Vikramathanvi, Adv.
          Mr. Chitrangda Rastravara, Adv.
          Mr. Celeste Agarwal, Adv.
          Ms. Manisha Chava, Adv.
          Mr. B. L. N. Shivani, Adv.
          Mr. Manvendra Singh, Adv.
          Mr. Aman Sharma, Adv.
          Mr. Arvind Kumar Sharma, AOR
          Mr. Bhuvan Mishra, Adv.

Mr. Naresh Kaushik, Adv.
Mr. Vardhman Kaushik , AOR
Mr. Dhruv Joshi, Adv.
Mr. Manoj Joshi, Adv.
Mr. Yogesh Yadav, Adv.
Mr. Anand Singh, Adv.
Mr. Prafful Saini, Adv.
Mr. Nishant Gautam, Adv.
Mr. B. Purushottama Reddy, Adv.
Mr. Lalitha Kaushik, AOR
Ms. Elaisha Asher, Adv.
Ms. Akshata Singh, Adv.
Mr. Manish Sharma , AOR
Ms. Divya Roy, AOR

UPON hearing the counsel the Court made the following
ORDER

Mrs. Aishwarya Bhati, learned ASG rightly points out that in a prophetic sense, the matter has come up on International Women's day.

We have perused the affidavit filed on behalf of the respondents in pursuance to the Order dated 18.1.2022.

We may notice the following aspects which emerge from the affidavit:-

a) the respondents need about 3 months time for deliberations to workout the implications in the long term of induction and deployment of ex-NDA women cadets into the Indian Armed Forces.

b) 5,75,854 candidates applied for the examination. 3,57,197 candidates took the examination. 8009 candidates including 1002 women candidates passed the NDA written examination held in November, 2021 and the Service Selection Board (SSB) is scheduled from March-April, 2022.

c) On the aspect of induction of women for NDA-II 2021 and NDA-I 2022, each course at NDA has 370 vacancies for the three services. 208 cadets get commissioned in the Indian Army, 120 cadets get commissioned in the Indian Air Force and 42 cadets in Indian Navy.

d) Insofar as the Indian Army is concerned, as per Ajai Vikram Singh Committee recommendations, the officer cadre is guided by 'regular cadre' to 'support cadre' ratio of 1:1.1. The nitty-gritty need not be referred by us.

e) Total vacancies planned for Indian Army through NDA is 416 every year i.e. 208 per course. Officers commissioned through NDA have a major component of the Combat Arms. Women Officers (WOs) are not being inducted in combat arms. 10 women candidates per NDA course are to be taken in, amounting to 11% of the earmarked vacancies.

f) The average intake in the last four years of women officers in the eight arms and services across the board has been upto 15% of the total cadre strength and with the present allotment of 10 women candidates per course in NDA i.e. 20 per year, the women cadre in these arms will witness a growth of 5% i.e. from the existing 15% to 20%.

g) A comparative chart of western armies and regional countries with percentage of enrolled women is given, keeping in mind that presently in the Indian Defence Forces, the women officers (including Army Medical Corps (AMC) and Military Nursing Service (MNS), an auxiliary force) constitute 13.6% of the officers' cadre. Illustratively, in some of the countries the figure is as under:-

	% of Women	Women Enrolled since
Australia	16.5	1899
USA	17	1898
France	15	1914
UK	11	1902
Germany	12	1975
Russia	10	1917
China	4.5	NK
Pakistan	2	2006
Myanmar	0.2	2014

Nepal	7	1962
Sri Lanka	2	1979

h) Training ethos of NDA being kept in mind, infrastructure is being developed and it is expected that the training of women candidates in NDA may attract foreign friendly countries to send their women candidates for training.

i) the position in Indian Navy is slightly different as all cadets inducted through UPSC Examination Post 10+2 into NDA are trained towards Executive (General Service) which is not open for induction of women officers. In fact, the Navy does not have any direct induction of men and women through NDA (UPSC) entry post 10+2. However, Navy has decided to induct women into three Branches/Cadres through NDA i.e. Education, Logistics and Naval Armament Inspectorate (NAI) Cadre. Navy has decided, keeping in mind the direction of this Court, to have intake of women as Permanent Commission (PC) officers through UPSC examinations in the aforesaid three branches. This is stated to be the first instance (whether for male or female) that a cadet will be trained at NDA for direct induction as PC officer in these three branches as at present no PC male officer is being directly inducted into these branches through NDA.

j) Women are stated to be already being trained in Indian Naval Academy at par with male cadets for commissioning in the Branches/Cadres which are open for their induction. Thus, induction of women into Indian Navy through UPSC 10+2 exam is not felt necessary. On an average 20 to 25 women are being inducted every six months for all Branches/ Cadres which are open for their induction.

k) 19 women candidates per term are being inducted at NDA which will after three years be about 114 women candidates. Upon passing from NDA, such of the candidates are inducted as Naval cadets who report at the Indian Naval Academy for Navy specific training for 6-12 months. So, these women cadet trainees are also being routed through Indian Navy.

l) The best picture which emerges is from the Indian Air Force as the women are being inducted in all its branches and sub-streams. The study carried out in 2013, and in 2021 are being used as the basis to arrive at the proposed IAF vacancies for women in NDA. With the proposed induction, 12 PC women officers will be inducted per year and will result in 60 PC women officers being inducted in the IAF over the next five years.

RASHTRIYA INDIAN MILITARY COLLEGE (RIMC)

The affidavit in compliance of Order dated 22.9.2021, which was affirmed on 06.10.2021 states that the admission into the RIMC is to be done through an All India Competitive Examination held biannually in June and December every year. States and Union Territories have been alloted one seat each except the States of Maharashtra, West Bengal and Tamil Nadu which have been allotted two seats and the State of Uttar Pradesh which has been alloted three seats. It was stated in the affidavit that to facilitate induction of the girls, there is a need for authorising additional vacancies along with the other associated infrastructure and administrative support through two phases which were set out in the affidavit.

We, however, directed that the course of action followed for NDA should also be followed for RIMC i.e. permitting women candidates to appear in terms of our Order dated 07.10.2021. That order has been complied with and learned ASG submits that 5 additional vacancies have been created for induction of women candidates.

The aforesaid arrangement having been made, I. A. No. 106572/2021 stands disposed of and we expect the process to continue.

RASHTRIYA MILITARY SCHOOLS (RMS)

RMS are English medium residential Public Schools. Five of them are spread across the country as "All Boys School" and act as a feeder institution for National Defence Academy to provide quality education and training to the wards of the Indian soldiers. 30% of the available seats are earmarked for wards of civilians and defence officers and the admission test is held in December for 350 seats. The induction was proposed in phase 1 & 2. No interim orders were passed but the affidavit records the assurance that the induction of women will begun from the academic session 2022-2023 which is taken on record.

SAINIK SCHOOLS

The Sainik Schools' experiment began with only induction of boys but subsequently some girls were inducted on experimental basis. That experiment was found fruitful as per the learned ASG and Hon'ble Prime Minister had made assurances from the ramparts of the Red Fort on 15th August, 2021 that there would be regular induction of girls. However, the exact data is to be submitted by learned ASG.

List on 19th July, 2022.

We appreciate the constructive approach being adopted by the Armed Services and assistance being rendered by the learned ASG not only as a law officer but as a woman.